Whatever You Do,
Don't Run

{ *True Tales of a*
Botswana Safari Guide }

Whatever You Do,
Don't Run

{ *True Tales of a*
Botswana Safari Guide }

Peter Allison

THE LYONS PRESS

An imprint of The Globe Pequot Press

The Lyons Press is an imprint of The Globe Pequot Press.

First Edition/Second Printing

Printed in the United States of America

All photos are by the author unless otherwise noted.
Text design by Lisa Reneson
Map created by Lisa Reneson © Morris Book Publishing, LLC

Library of Congress Cataloging-in-Publication Data
Allison, Peter.
  Whatever you do, don't run : true tales of a Botswana safari guide / Peter Allison.
— 1st ed.
    p. cm.
  ISBN: 978-0-7627-4565-4
  1. Allison, Peter. 2. Safari guides—Botswana—Biography. 3. Safaris—Botswana—Anecdotes. I. Title.
  G156.A45 2007
  916.88304'32092—dc22
  [B]
                                        2007005094

This book is dedicated to anyone who works to protect wild places and the animals within them, but in particular to the safari guides who taught me so much.

My particular thanks go to Chris Greathead, Devlin Foxcroft, Iain Garrett, the Marais family (including Sally), Helen Dewar, Duncan Menzies, Alpheus Mathebula, Titus Indloovu, B.K. Setlabosha, Lloyd Camp, Clinton "Cliffy" Phillips, Grant Woodrow, Mike Myers, Lex Hes, Richard Field, Paul Allen, Colin Bell, Russell Friedman, Chris Kruger, Julius Masogo, the late great Rantaung Rantaung, and the sadly missed Nandi Retiyo.

Everything I know about animals I learned from this group, so any mistakes in this book are their fault.

Contents

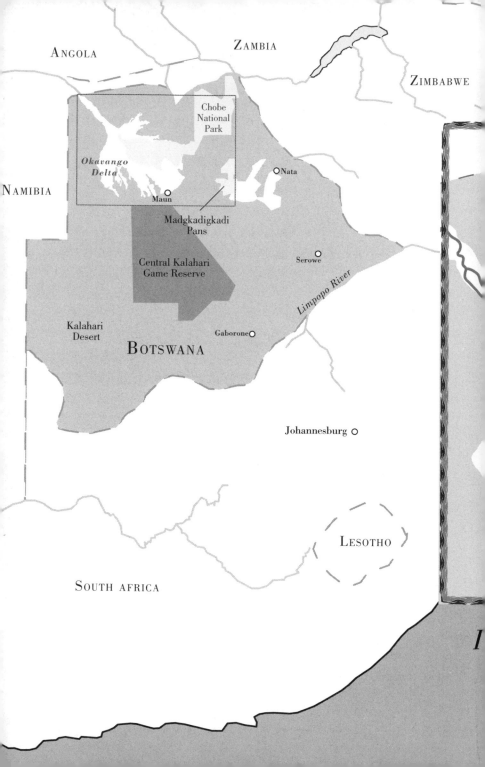

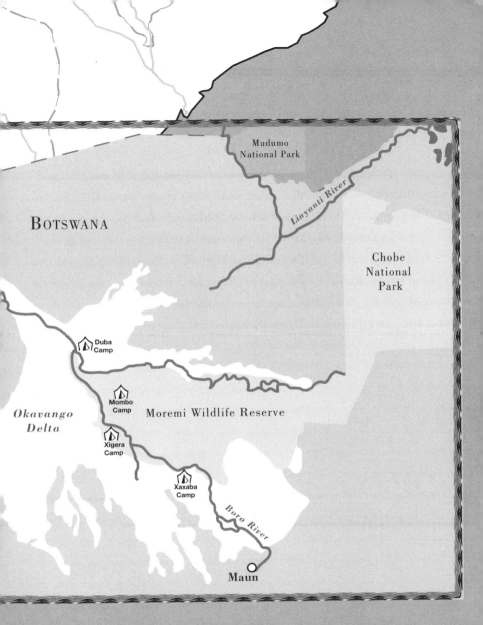

Mudumo
National Park

BOTSWANA

Linyanti River

Chobe
National
Park

Duba
Camp

Mombo
Camp

Moremi Wildlife Reserve

Okavango
Delta

Xigera
Camp

Xaxaba
Camp

Boro River

Maun

ndian Ocean

Acknowledgments

This book couldn't have been written without the able assistance and encouragement of a wonderful group of women. Without Flavia I would never have had the courage to start this book, let alone finish it. My sister Laurie was subjected to some of the earliest drafts without visibly wincing. Without my magnificent agent and friend, Kate, I would never have found a home for the book and met Laura, Imee, Gail, Jaclyn, and Katie at Globe Pequot. To all of you I give many, many thanks.

When I was nineteen, after two years in a job that was going nowhere, I bought a ticket and set off for Africa. I went for two reasons. First, I wanted a challenge. And second, all of my life I have loved and been fascinated by wildlife. My plan was to stay for only a year.

After six months of backpacking in Africa, I had spent most of my money and the rest had been stolen at a Malawian campground. This helped fulfill the criteria of a challenge. Kindly fellow travelers offered to drive me to South Africa, where I could arrange for more funds. During our journey we stopped at a game reserve.

At the end of two astonishing days, which I spent in a state of euphoria, my obvious enthusiasm was rewarded with an offer to run the bar at the camp. Happily putting down my backpack, and cutting off my long hair, I accepted.

Living in the bush was more than I had ever expected was possible. I had grown up in the most sedate suburbs, and in my own mind I had none of the qualities you would expect of a rugged bush man. I'm markedly uncoordinated, can't repair vehicles nor understand how they work, I don't like guns, and sweat profusely when nervous or excited—which is exactly how watching animals makes me feel.

Nevertheless over time I advanced in position and became a guide, then a camp manager, then a teacher for others who wished to become guides. My short holiday to Africa has been keeping me busy since 1994, and I don't foresee it ever ending.

These are the stories from the life of a safari guide.

Whatever You Do, Don't Run

The first place in Africa that employed me was a camp called Idube. The people who came there, like the people who came to every camp where I have ever worked, loved a thrill, something different. So we took them out to dinner.

Not far from our main camp we had a small setup, inventively called the Bush Camp. It included a teepee over a toilet and a clearing where a fire could be built. Around this, chairs and tables were set, ready for the delighted guests who would be brought in the dark for their meal. Firelight is romantic and makes everyone look beautiful, just as it did for the Bush Camp. With lanterns lit and a beaming staff, the place looked perfect. But during the day it was only a sorry patch of earth, and the teepee was filled with spiders. The guests loved it, and the nights were cheap for the camp's owners, so they insisted we run them at least once a week.

The staff didn't like these dinner nights in the bush. Setting up meant that the usual quiet time, when all the guests were out of camp, was suddenly filled with frantic activity. The one spare Land Rover, a decrepit and spluttering machine called the Skorokoro (which means "too old to work" in Shangaan), would be loaded with firewood, lanterns, and a chef named Wusani, whose bulk always made the aging suspension creak ominously. Wusani particularly disliked these bush dinners, as one afternoon after being dropped off she was unpleasantly surprised. Shortly after she lit the cooking fire, a lion roared, according to her description, "closer to me than a baby is to its mother." Lions often walked in the soft sand of the dry riverbed that flowed beside the Bush Camp, to enjoy the shade or maybe to startle an antelope that had been lulled to sleep by the cool and tranquility of the surrounds. This lion was not hunting, or it would not have roared, but that didn't make it any less terrifying for Wusani.

When the Skorokoro and its driver returned that day with the tables and chairs, they found Wusani improbably perched on the outermost branches of a long-dead tree. When told it was safe to come down, she would not, because she could not. Adrenaline had fueled the climb, and now she only had the strength to cling on and beg for a ladder that the camp did not possess.

Finally gravity's pull resolved the issue. Despite her substantial weight and the height she fell from, Wusani was saved from serious harm—perhaps by her ample padding. But she would never stay at the Bush Camp by herself again, and she warned me against it when I started working at Idube.

My job for bush dinners was simpler than Wusani's. I had to transport sufficient amounts of alcohol to the Bush Camp to last the night. I hadn't been working at the camp long, and as barman I was probably the most lowly staff member after the "gardener," who watered the lawns that the warthogs promptly dug up. This gave me last priority when it came to loading the Skorokoro.

"Bugger it," I thought one afternoon when I had already

helped load tables, chairs, cloths, salads, and cutlery to the exclusion of the booze. "I'll carry it there."

Animals were the last things on my mind as I loaded up a wheelbarrow with spirits and mixers. All I wanted was to get my job done. Besides, I'd been learning from the guides and felt that I was getting to be reasonably bush smart. With the cockiness of a nineteen-year-old, I felt I could handle anything that Africa threw at me. Whenever an animal encounter of the sort I was about to have was discussed, the advice was always the same: "Whatever you do, don't run." This was the solemn counsel of the three guides who worked at the camp. "Food runs," added Alpheus, the tracker, his rough face split by an enormous grin. "And there is nothing here that you can outrun anyway."

After grunting and sweating my way along the sandy tracks that the Land Rovers used, I dropped off my first load and trudged back. All that I needed to take to the Bush Camp now was a case of beer. Filled with bravado, I decided to ditch the wheelbarrow and carry the drinks instead. I hadn't considered how heavy twenty-four cans of beer gets when you are slogging through soft sand for almost a mile. Only a quarter of the way into my journey, I decided to change routes and take a shortcut along the riverbed.

At one point I stopped to shake a small pebble from my shoe. Quartz, I concluded, because it was the only rock type I knew. I rested, gently putting the beer down and stretching. Branches met overhead, offering cool shade and a sense of peace that mingled with the constant undercurrent of excitement that comes from walking in the bush. In one of the branches, a type of bird named the grey lourie called, a long drawn out rasp that sounds like a hag telling you to go away. "Ka—weeeeeeeeeeeee." It is not an emphatic sound, but it is irritatingly insistent. Later I would learn that this is just one of the many birds that give an alarm call when it sees a predator. The tricky part is figuring out whether it is saying it because of you (after all, humans are Africa's most abundant predator) or because of something larger and fiercer.

I put my shoe back on, hopping around to do so; picked up the beer; and rounded a fallen log. This startled two massive male lions that had been waiting for whatever clumsy creature was making all the noise, probably expecting a buffalo.

They may have leapt to their feet, they may have flown. I don't know because it was so fast I didn't see. The time it took for them to get from where they were to where I stood was too short for my life to flash before my eyes. Instead I skipped to a day in December, when I was seven years old.

Our next-door neighbors had a German shepherd named Pancho. Pancho scared the crap out of me. On the few occasions that we had been inside their house, he would pace a circuit from the kitchen through the living room to the dining room and round again, dipping his head to a canine rhythm and growling.

On this day, my mother, sister, and I were going to Hawaii so my mother could run in the Honolulu marathon. She was doing this even though she was sick, because she was a proud and determined woman and wanted it done. She was sick enough that while she completed the marathon, it would be the only overseas trip my sister and I would ever get to take with her. The medicines that customs would not allow, and I now carried next door for our neighbor to safeguard while we were away, would prove useless, and cancer would take her within a year.

The lady of the house was on the front lawn, brushing Pancho while holding him by the collar. Afterward my father, who considered himself an animal expert, would state that Pancho must have mistaken the medicine in my pudgy fist as a weapon. I was always convinced that the motive was much more simple— hatred. Pancho hated everyone except his owners, and here I was, coming like a sacrifice.

To get to me, he violently twisted his neck, breaking his collar and leaving it in his owner's grip. My father had always said to me that if a dog attacked (and even before that December day, I knew he must have been warning me about Pancho), that whatever I did, I mustn't run. I had always imagined that if a dog (all right, if Pancho) did attack me, it was my mother I would make proud by standing bravely. She had also warned me about animals, and in a rare case of agreement, had repeated my father's words: "Whatever you do, don't run."

I ran. As fast as my little seven-year-old legs could whir, I ran for the low brick fence, insanely convinced that if I could just clear it, Pancho would stop at the boundary set out by some long-forgotten property surveyors. I could hear his owner shouting, "Pancho, no!" and "Pancho, come back!" so I must have outpaced him for only as long as it takes to say those words. With the fence still agonizingly far away, he pulled me down and mauled me.

Twelve years later on another hot December day, I once again had every instinct telling me to run.

"Let's see if you've grown," was one of the only things I had time to think before the two lions were at me.

The other thing I thought, and it shames me to admit it, is

this: If you drop the beer, it will get all fizzed up. And which motive was the strongest, I don't know. But I stood my ground and gave my best attempt at a roar back at the lions.

The lions stopped. Only an arm's length away from me, they bellowed and spat and then, with a visible release of tension in their bodies, trotted around me and carried on down the riverbed as if they had pressing business elsewhere.

I put the case of beer in the sand and sat on it as a stool. I shook, and listened to the birds. I felt the fear that hadn't had the time to arrive earlier and let it wash over me. But through the fear I felt something else.

Pride.

The Lesson

"You should learn how to walk," Chris said to me.

I was nineteen and had been getting around on two feet with relative ease for some years, so the comment might have seemed strange to an outsider. But we were in a safari camp, and the walking Chris was talking about would involve in-depth knowledge of trees, tracks, insects, and all the smaller things that were usually overlooked on a safari drive. I had only recently been offered the chance to become a guide and was doing my best to absorb the knowledge and skills required.

There was the possibility that on one of these walks that I, and the tourists that I was being trained to lead, would inadvertently find one of the larger, more dangerous animals that we hoped to see only from the safety of a vehicle. In this case it was important that I had the ability to remain calm—and not run.

Because of this it was important to make sure that if something did charge, I "had what it took." This was safari-speak for having the ability to stand your ground against something that was hurtling at you with the full capability and possible intent of eating you. There is no point trying to outrun any of the dangerous animals in Africa anyway. Humans are almost laughably slow, not able to outpace even the obese hippo, the top-heavy giraffe, or the surprisingly sprightly warthog.

Iain, one of the guides training me, used to tell a joke at mealtimes about this lack of speed: Two guys are out walking when they see a lion, and it starts stalking them. One of the guys kicks off his hiking boots, reaches into a backpack, whips out some running shoes, and starts lacing them up. "What are you doing?" the other asks. "You can't outrun a lion."

"I don't need to," comes the reply. "I only have to outrun you."

The joke always got a laugh, so it was recycled with almost every group that passed through. I heard it plenty of times before I ever got close to a lion on foot, so it came to the forefront of my mind when Chris walked into the camp office carrying a rifle.

"There are lions right outside camp," he said. "It's the Ravenscourt Pride. They're a bit nasty at times." This was an understatement. They were the prime suspects in a man-eating case from a year earlier. "It's been a while since I faced a charge. I want to see if I've still got it."

I wasn't sure if my one experience with lions counted, as I suspected it was fear and not confidence that had rooted me to the ground. "I'd like to come along, and see if I've got it at all," I piped up.

Then I poked Chris in his not-quite-flat belly. "Besides which, I reckon I could outrun you."

Chris didn't comment at first. He just put some rounds in the rifle, then chambered one. He smiled benevolently at me. "Not with a bullet in your leg."

I watched his smile to see if it wavered, some indication that he was joking. But he held it admirably firm, and I was somewhat relieved when after an hour or so of tracking we decided the lions had moved away. I would have to wait for another day to see if I had what it took to be a guide.

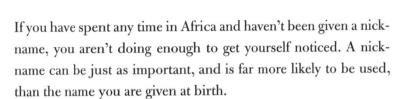

How I Got My Name

If you have spent any time in Africa and haven't been given a nickname, you aren't doing enough to get yourself noticed. A nickname can be just as important, and is far more likely to be used, than the name you are given at birth.

The people I worked with in South Africa were mainly from the Shangaan tribe and were considered the masters of getting right to a person's essence and defining it with one or two words. The couple who owned our camp, and were not always loved by the staff, were known as "Mamba Eyes" for her and "June/July" for him—a reference to the South African winter months and the way the staff felt a chill when they saw him.

I waited eagerly for a moniker, sure that since I was a nice guy I would be treated well. If I caught a staff member looking at me with the slightest hint of assessment, I would try my best to act as serene as the Dalai Lama, as kindly as Santa, and as cool as Elvis in the hope of being called something like "That Hip Guy From Far Away" or "Number One Sexy Beast." Most likely I came across as constipated, but it was irrelevant, as the assessing look often turned out to be a warm-up for a request for a loan until payday. I was then faced with the dilemma of rejecting them (unbeknownst to them I was one of the lowest-paid people in the camp, making about four dollars a day) and getting a name like "Cheap Bastard," or coughing up the cash and being known as "Rollover" or "Soft Touch"—either of which had disturbing double meanings that I was sensitive about since I was lonely on the romantic front. There were no single girls in camp, and my fumbling attempts at seducing guests were rejected because they only had eyes for the guides and I was only the barman. And all the alcohol at my disposal couldn't make the animals attractive.

In the end it was this missing element in my life that decided the name for me. Titus, one of the trackers, called me one day by shouting "Ngwenza! Gunjaan?" I only understood the second word, which means "How are you?" So I asked the chef, a kindly woman named Rosie, what *Ngwenza* meant. She snorted into the bread she was mixing and said, "Is that your name?"

"I think so. What does it mean?"

She wouldn't tell. I asked Harold, the gardener. He reeked of marijuana, and I was sure that he was taking better care of a garden somewhere else than he was of the lawn in the camp. As soon as I said the word *Ngwenza*, he went into high hysterics, fell on all fours, thumped the brown grass, and said, "Yes! That is you!" He wouldn't, or possibly couldn't, tell me anymore, so I left him with his grass and went in search of an answer elsewhere.

Eventually I asked Alpheus, the camp's other tracker what *Ngwenza* meant. His pitted face split into a grin, and he said in his rough voice, "A man who has not been with a woman for a long, long time."

"You mean sexually frustrated? That's my name?"

There was no point arguing it. I guessed that doing so

would only reinforce it. Anyway, it could only be a matter of time before I gave the name reason to be changed—I hoped.

The name did change, but not for the reason I wanted it to. One of the impediments I faced in becoming a guide was that I didn't know how to drive. I'd left home too early to have my parents teach me, and I never could have afforded driving school. The guides declared that I knew enough about the animals, birds, and trees to start guiding, if I only knew how to get a Land Rover around on the rough tracks—and off them when following something like a cheetah as it hunted. They took me out in turns. Chris, the most knowledgeable, gave up after I scraped the side of the vehicle while getting it out of its bay. Iain, who I was closest to, grew quickly frustrated at my inability to master the clutch, brake, accelerator, and four-wheel drive select knob in one go. To my surprise it was Devlin (known to the staff as "19" because of a missing finger), a party animal and genital exhibitionist, who was the best teacher. He was patient, and good at explaining the process that occurred as gears meshed and released and fuel was applied, but most important he took me to a place where I could do the least amount of damage.

Unlike the open plains shown in many documentaries, the South African bush is fairly dense and scrubby, so the places to practice were few. Devlin drove us to a clearing that had one tree in it, inventively called One Tree Plain, surrounded by open grassland. Along the way we had to stop and clear a tree that had been pushed across the road by an elephant. Elephants push over trees for two reasons. The first is for food—to eat the leaves at the very top of the tree or to get at the exposed roots. This tree, though, had not been fed on, so it was apparent that the culprit was a bull who was filled with testosterone but no outlet for it, so he pushed over trees. It's a great release for a bull and a way of showing his strength after a female has rejected him. If human males had the same ability, global deforestation would be complete by now.

After moving the fallen tree, we carried on to One Tree Plain and the driving class. By the end of my lesson, the name of the area had to be changed to No Tree Plain, and the vehicle sported a conspicuous dent in the bumper guard.

I had futilely hoped that Devlin might not tell anyone, but it was apparent that he had because the staff stopped calling me Ngwenza, and added a postscript. I was now "Ngwenza Indloovu," the "Sexually Frustrated Elephant." I was never addressed as anything else. And even after months had passed, cackling still accompanied any mention of my new name.

I finally left South Africa to move north, and the name didn't follow me across the tribal and political border into Botswana. But on a return visit after many years, the staff I still knew snorted as they greeted me as Ngwenza. As I squatted to have a bush tea with Titus (whose last name really is Indloovu), he asked if I was being lucky (a colloquial phrase that doesn't require the addition of "with women" to be clear).

"Sure," I said. "I'm a guide now."

"Naaah," he drawled out the word. "You're still Ngwenza."

"Ngwenza Indloovu, you mean," I corrected him, but smiling as I did.

"Sure," he said, mimicking me. "Ngwenza."

Maybe it was because I wasn't nineteen anymore, or maybe it was because I knew that there were worse things that I could be called, but I didn't mind my name at all. We drank our tea, I asked after his family, and he told me who had left, who had died, and what the animals I used to know were doing. He told me that Bombi the leopard was dead, but Uncle One-Horn the rhino still held his territory.

I'd learned a lot more about Africa and its customs in the years I had been away, so I asked him about his cattle and whether he was expecting to be blessed with any more sons. When I left, he shook my hand and bid me farewell using the name he had given me, and as improbable as it may seem, he made it sound respectful.

The Great Mouse Plague

I left the relative safety of South Africa after two years working at Idube, and went in search of more experience, more knowledge, and a wilder adventure.

Knowing very little about Botswana, except that my friend and mentor Chris was working there, I moved north and settled into the Okavango Delta. The Delta is the world's largest oasis in the world's largest stretch of sand, and I was based on the largest island in it. Whereas the camp I had worked for in South Africa was made of brick and mortar and connected to the outside world by decent (if dirt) roads and had luxuries like a telephone line, my new home in Botswana was reachable only by air, communicated with the outside world by a crackly radio, and was built out of timber and canvas. In my first year through a combination of bravado and greenness, I got the experience I was after—and maybe a little more knowledge. Living among wild animals ensured that I would also have adventure. What I hadn't predicted is what sort of animal would provide most of it.

As the year drew to a close, the annual rains came to Northern Botswana. There was a little more rain than usual, but nothing extraordinary enough to foretell what was coming.

What those of us living in the Okavango didn't know was that just enough had fallen for the grass to make huge amounts of seeds without them getting so soaked that they would rot. We were just as unaware that the grass was the perfect length for mice to make nests, then breed again, and again, and again. By the time the rains were drawing to an end in March, we knew we had a problem. People came to Africa for the wildlife, but as they remarked with great frequency, the list of animals they wished to see did not include mice. They could go to Anaheim for that, they'd add, not realizing that we didn't know what they meant (only years later would I see a map of Disneyland and say, "OK, now I get it").

But see the mice they did. They were inescapable. Our food stores were overrun—they even ate the laces out of shoes and tore up clothes to pad their homes.

Although the mice were usually nocturnal, by March the bush started to dry up and their natural food dwindled, so they had to stay out longer to forage. In the mornings as I made my way to wake the guests, the mice would move ahead of me in waves. And as I shone my flashlight in the strengthening light, I would see them closing ranks behind me again, forming a moving carpet of fur.

This abundance made the predators happy, as were some of the smaller herbivores whose normal enemies were so heavily gorged they were barely capable of movement. Jackals, wildcats, owls, mongoose, genets, servals, and even leopard swatted away at the ground without taking serious aim. But the predation didn't dent the population.

Eventually the mice ran out of food on the ground and were seen stripping shrubs and even trees of anything edible. Nothing was beyond their reach. It was like we were living in the Old Testament and had pissed off God.

I suggested that someone brave radio the office in Maun and tell them to either shut the camp no matter what the cost or let the incoming people know that they would be sharing their tent with some hungry invaders. We'd just had the third case of a mouse overdosing on a guest's malaria pills, which would have been funny if I hadn't seen the mouse in question on its back in a toiletries bag draw its last few desperate breaths. By then mice were the only exception to my love of all things animal, yet I still didn't like seeing them die.

The dead mouse did give me the opportunity, though, to identify the species that was plaguing us. My colleagues told me that I was obsessive compulsive, but it was only my first year in Botswana. Despite a confident air that I put on, I was still unsure of myself and keen to impress. So I pored over a book, deciding the deceased was too large to be a desert pygmy mouse, was out at night so was not a single striped mouse, and was not chubby enough to be a fat mouse (the species' real name). Eventually, triumphantly, I declared it to be a common pouched mouse, at which my colleagues congratulated me mockingly and declared me a nerd.

"How can you be sure—don't all mice look the same?" Chloe asked.

"Because I'm never wrong," I answered cockily, stealing a line from my friend Devlin. Then changing the subject I explained more about the mice. "It says here that a female can breed every five weeks, having as many as seven babies."

My colleagues grunted to show how much they cared.

"The young are ready to breed when only four weeks old. One mouse can produce something like ten thousand descendants in the space of a few months."

"Maybe you should stop sleeping with them then," Grant replied.

"Maybe you should radio the office. It's only going to get worse."

■ ■

Since Grant was the manager, he finally called to say that we were overrun. Our Maun office told us they would handle our problem with the mice. We waited, curious to see what they would do. When the next plane came in to drop off tourists and supplies, they'd sent a mouse trap. Not just any mouse trap, but an ecofriendly one. This was a little two-story cage that caught the mice alive so they could be relocated.

"No way," Grant said. "I don't think they understand the scope of this."

We were almost 90 miles away, but we often felt as if we were on another planet from the people in the office. Somehow we needed to make them understand.

That night we put some peanut butter (a far better mouse bait than cheese) in the lower tier. As we watched, a mouse approached and climbed the access door to the top level. He ran along inside the cage, until he hit a spring loaded hatch that dropped him to the lower level, at which point the hatch sprang back, trapping him on the lower section. Another mouse followed almost immediately. By morning the cage was so full that mice were pressed hard up against the bars of their prison. Without emptying it, we put the trap into the mailbag and returned it to the office.

They sent it back, empty, with a note, addressed from the office cat, simply saying, "Thanks." We decided it was to be a war of attrition, so set the trap again. The first guide to come out in the morning found the cage full again, but with the mice backed in abject terror against one side. There was a cobra whose head and first third were in the cage with them. To the snake the cage must have looked like a buffet, and it had slithered in, only to find that when it swallowed its victims they stuck in its gullet where the bars were pinching. From the lumps we deduced it had swallowed three before possible indigestion or a tail tickling its throat made it stop. Nobody wanted to pull it out, so we picked the whole thing up, stuck it in the mailbag, and sent it away again, the cobra hissing angrily. This time when the office returned it empty, it didn't have a thank-you note.

As winter approached, the grass started to die back, reducing the cover for the mice and exposing them to aerial predators. It was spectacular to see a sky filled with hawks, eagles, and kestrels, many of which had delayed their return to Europe to swoop and gorge on the abundant prey. It felt like the mice numbers were dropping, only because the times you were woken at night by an animal scurrying over you was reduced to three or four. We were sure that we had won the rodent war.

What we didn't factor in while we did our victory dance was the very thing that makes the Okavango Delta so special. Every year it floods—but during the dry season. There is a river in Angola that fills at the same time it is raining in Botswana. As it meanders south it is abruptly diverted away from the coast and into the desert by a fault line, creating the world's largest oasis. As the rest of the Kalahari withers in the dry winter months, the Okavango springs back into life.

It is an annual tradition to watch this flood come in. First the channels fill, then their banks are breached and the flood infiltrates the plains. The land is so flat that the clear water creeps as slowly as molasses, creating vast shallow water plains and small islands of trees. It is possible to stand and watch the water edge slowly toward you, but this year the edge of the flood was occupied. From a distance it looked like an oil field, with rigs bobbing up and down, the difference being that these rigs were taking a step back every few minutes. Through binoculars we saw that it was more marabou storks than any of us had ever seen before, literally thousands of them. They are one of the world's largest birds, standing over four feet tall, and also one of the world's most unattractive. They have a balding head complete with liver spots and the occasional bedraggled feather. Beneath their throat hangs an obscene-looking pink pouch that for reasons unknown to science they inflate on occasion, making it look very much like they have some sort of malformed genital under their beak—and a big one at that.

The storks were eating the mice—watching the water as it crept in and filled the burrows, then nabbing the mice as they ran out. In the air above them, buzzards circled, grabbing some of the ones that had made it past the skirmish line. Even from a distance we knew there were nowhere near enough birds to catch all the mice, and the thousands that escaped would be looking for higher ground and the dry land it offered. Like the place where our camp was built.

"Bugger," I said. "They're coming."

If we thought we'd had a problem earlier, now it was tenfold. Every surface was like a living thing, swarming with the rodent refugees. As an experiment one night I took off my boot as I got into bed and threw it into the corner of my tent. It killed two mice. The other boot got only one. The mice were desperately hungry and were eating everything. They ate the plastic that seals the refrigerator doors shut, then ate everything inside, even frozen meat. They chewed through the canvas of our tents and ate first the leather of our belts and boots, then started on the dry fibers of our clothes.

Their fearlessness grew to epic proportions. I watched a lion, apparently driven mad, chasing his tail, then I realized there was a mouse clinging to its tip. Elephants confirmed something that I had always thought to be a myth: They are frightened of mice. Through the day and night you would hear the occasional anguished squeal from the true king of beasts as a mouse would run over its trunk. I'm sure they squashed many mice just by walking around, but nothing seemed to be reducing the plague. Even while starving, the mice felt compelled to copulate, and I kept finding thin ribbed couples taking a break from foraging to fornicate.

Some evenings I heard the sound that every camp manager and guide fears. In each guest tent was a gas-powered siren, which we emphatically explained was for medical or animal emergency use only. In more than ten years of safaris I have still heard the sirens less than a dozen times. Four of these were because of mice. One was for a small fire, started when a mouse chewed through the rubber coating on a wire that powered a small lantern in the room. The other three times, and by now we were all so exhausted as to find this funny, was because of bald men. The mice developed a penchant for the dark sun spots that some bald men have on their heads—nobody had a theory as to why, but the managers spent many nighttime hours apologizing on behalf of our company for the behavior of the wildlife.

Some people demanded refunds, and we sympathized, because chewing on bald men was not the most disgusting thing the mice were doing. Oh no, that came when they were really hungry and anything that smelled was considered a potential source of food. Imagine the discomfort it causes waking up with a mouse trying to crawl into the smelliest part of your body. (It took the staff years to admit to each other that at some stage we had all experienced this, and we wondered how many guests had been just too embarrassed to mention it.)

As I was a guide and not a camp manager, most complaints were not directed to me. On game drives we were still seeing the abundance of life that the Okavango has to offer, and that pleased most people. It only became personal when, because of the mice, I made the worst animal misidentification in the history of Africa. This history goes back a rather long way.

We had a full camp of twenty people, but I was taking out only a family of four on drives, because it included two teenage daughters that other camps had warned us were "difficult." We decided that since we were asking the other sixteen people in the camp to tolerate our little rodent infestation, we should not inflict a couple of California brats on them while they were trying to enjoy the wildlife.

So I endured the family alone.

The teenage girls were both of the age that they craved

attention, but they were not yet mature enough to use their feminine charms to get it. Instead they were "afraid" of everything. I'm quite sure they were punishing their father for dragging them all the way to Africa for a holiday, instead of letting them hang out at the mall with their friends like they would have, like, liked.

On drives they would flinch away from every insect. "Is it poisonous? Does it bite? Does it sting?"

"It's a dung beetle. All it does is seek out and home in on crap," I answered. The father smirked at this; the mother didn't.

When we saw lions, the girls gripped each other and wailed, "They're going to jump in the car and kill us all!"

Safaris in Botswana don't use closed vans like they do in Kenya. We had Land Rovers with the top lopped off. I explained that if the animals were in the habit of leaping in, we might change our policy on that.

"You've always got a smart answer," the older sister said. "You think you know everything."

"Naaaah," I drawled the word. "I don't even come close to knowing everything…" I was smiling, perhaps a little cocky because it was so rare for me to deal with clients younger than myself, " . . . but I'm never wrong."

■ ▩

On their last night in the camp, the family stood as one after dinner to head to their tents. Every evening we escorted people to their rooms in case there was an animal on the path. Taking the "Torture Twins" had been a teeth-grinding nightmare on the two previous evenings, but as I was their guide it was my responsibility.

I grabbed three flashlights—one for the parents, one for the girls, and the last for me.

We ate dinner every night on a raised deck, and as soon as we stepped off it you could hear the rustle of mice moving, searching, feeding. The fake whimpers started, and I set off at a faster pace than I usually would take in the dark. My flashlight swung from left to right, illuminating the path and anything that might be lurking beside it. Behind me another beam stayed resolutely at our feet, and I presumed this was the father's. The last beam flitted through the night sky, whipped around and behind us, then up and down, creating a disco effect. The girl. Maybe she was looking for vampire bats.

Apart from the strobe light, the night sky was mainly clear, as it was almost every night in winter. Missing, though, was Scorpio, which should have been on the horizon, but it was obscured.

We'd taken maybe three dozen paces from the deck and were about to walk under the canopy of a rain tree when there was a rustle in front us.

"Oh my god oh my god oh my god is it going to kill us?"

"It's a mouse. It's only a mouse. They're bloody everywhere," I said crankily.

At that, a branch on the tree shook violently.

And I saw tusks.

Then a trunk.

Then I realized that Scorpio was obscured by an elephant. They're big.

We were standing about three feet from it.

Oh my god oh my god oh my god, I thought. I guess I'm not always right.

"Let's head back to the deck," I said as calmly as I could, hoping that my voice hadn't really broken on the last syllable. "The elephants have been a little upset, what with all the mice."

We got back to the deck safely, the elephant standing perfectly still in the way that only an elephant can. The branch shake had just been a polite warning for us not to come any closer. This sort of courtesy from an animal astonishes people, but I was more amazed that neither girl had said anything about my obvious gaffe. Could they have missed it? Perhaps in that uniquely American way they had been hearing everything I'd said, but not listening. For the first time ever that thought comforted, rather than offended, me. The family would be leaving tomorrow, but I had to work with my colleagues for years, and they were just as keen as the girl was to see me make a mistake. Not out of any malice, but because it would give them a wonderful story to tell at my expense.

Within minutes I watched the older girl whisper darkly into the manager's ear. Damn.

Eventually the managers went to bed, and so did my guests, this time without incident. I pointed out Scorpio for no other reason than to show that I knew something. They didn't seem impressed. I went to my tent, still embarrassed. The mouse plague would end, as nature took its course, but the people I worked with would never forget my mistake and often started nights at the fire with, "Let me tell you about the time Peter almost got his guests killed, when he mistook an elephant for a mouse."

Deliverance

Chris liked Ella.

A lot.

Chris's confidence was a problem. Despite his impressive height and the physical presence that came with it, and despite being one of the best guides most people had ever met, he took forever to make his move. "Chris's seductions are slower than cancer," his brother Andrew told me grimly. "But nowhere near as deadly."

The two had hit it off though, after an excruciatingly long time, but they were still at the stage that Chris felt the need to convince Ella she hadn't made a dreadful mistake. As a camp manager he had had little opportunity to impress her with one of his greatest assets—his ability as a guide. When a friend of ours named Allison was visiting from another camp, he made a plan for us all to go on a night drive, in which he would take the wheel and show off his formidable bush knowledge.

With Chris driving, Ella in the passenger seat beside him, and Allison and I on the pewlike row behind them, huddled under a blanket against the winter chill, we set off for a place where the lions had been seen snoozing that afternoon. We hoped to catch them before they set off for the night and follow them hunting.

There were no guests with us, so we were speaking freely, and each of us had a drink in our hand. Allison and I were both aware that Chris was trying to be impressive, and we were aiding him by trying not to laugh when he told us things about the bush that we already knew.

We had left as the last light fled the sky and the crepuscular creatures crawled from their burrows. The remaining red in the sky bled out as we reached the place the lions had last been seen. We expected to catch them still sleeping, or up and slowly stretching, getting ready for their night of violence. But they were gone. We shone the spotlight around, scanning for the forms that would appear gray in the darkness.

There was nothing.

"Okay chaps," Chris said. (He called everyone "chaps.") "It's a bit naughty, but let's see if we can draw them out." His plan was to make the sound of a dying impala and attract the lions with it, as they are even happier than hyenas to steal a kill from another animal rather than hunt themselves. Calling them like this was on the border of unethical, because we didn't like to disturb any animal out making its living, but since they had only just got started and lions take a while to warm up, we all agreed that it wasn't too grievous an offense.

Chris shut off all the lights and killed the engine. Blackness enveloped the world, and I realized there was no moon.

"Blaaaaaaaaagh," went Chris. "Blaaaaaaaaaaaaagh! Blaaeeeeeeeeeeeeeeeeeaaaaaaaaaaaaaaaaaagh!"

It was the most ludicrous sound I had ever heard. The

strangled gargling sounded like a goat that was having an unpleasant sexual encounter.

"Bleeeeeeeeeagh!" continued Chris, and beside me I could feel Allison shaking with barely contained laughter. I began to chortle myself but pulled the blanket up over my mouth to muffle the sound.

My eyes had adjusted to the faint starlight that was our only illumination, and I could see that the surrounding plain was empty. Not even a hyena had been drawn by the feeble cries.

"I've got an idea Chris!" I said. "Squeal like a pig!"

Chris, still desperate to impress and show that he could summon lions at his command, switched to a high-pitched squeal, his six-foot-four frame expanding with air and slowly deflating as he let out his tortured death call.

"Qweeeeeeeee! Qwooooeeeeeeeeeeeeee!" A warthog dies with little vocal elegance, and Chris's squeal was equally as unpleasant to hear. "Qweeeeeeeeee!" he persisted admirably if unattractively, his voice cracking like a pubescent boy's. Now I saw that Ella too was vibrating with mirth, and a snort escaped me.

Somehow over his death call, Chris heard my own little pig noise and said, "What's so funny?" and we lost it. Ella, Allison, and I burst into raucous laughter while Chris sat looking wounded. He shot me a dark look. I'd agreed to back him up in his seduction efforts and was now laughing the loudest.

"Fine," he muttered, turning the key in the ignition and flinging on the headlights, illuminating a lioness that was within two feet of us.

In the thousands of hours I have spent watching lions, I have never felt that one was about to jump into the car, except this once. Her posture was low to the ground; she was definitely stalking. She was practically under our noses, and not one of us had seen her get there. There was a determined set to her face as she looked for a free meal from whatever was dying so noisily on the vehicle.

The laughter had stopped mid-chuckle, and we all sat dead still. I heard a click as Chris turned on the handheld spotlight, then he swung the beam of light into her face.

She batted her eyes, and her body relaxed. She rose fluidly from the low crouch she had been in, blinking and squinting at the light as if to say, "Aw come on, knock it off would ya, I'm looking for some bacon!" She walked around the vehicle once, sniffing and listening, saw nothing worth eating, and wandered away making the soft, low contact calls a lion uses when it is separated from its pride.

"That," I said to Chris, "was very impressive." And I meant it.

Clearly Ella thought so too, because a few years later she married him.

Buffalo School

When I first moved from South Africa to Botswana, I had to hit the books and prevail upon other guides to educate me about a number of things that were new to me. There were antelopes in the Okavango that I had never even seen before but was required to speak knowledgeably about. I would also face African wild dogs for the first time, and there were many types of obscure creatures that could only be found in the region as well.

One animal, though, would require the steepest learning curve—buffalo. The reserve that I had come from in South Africa was rather impoverished when it came to buffalo, and there were only three sad and lonely old bulls that lived in thick vegetation by the Sand River. I had seen them only a handful of times, from a distance as they sat deep in impenetrable reeds and always from the safe haven of a vehicle.

I did know a fair amount about buffalo from books, but I also knew that books were often too narrow in their definition of how an animal might behave. What the books did agree on was that old male buffalo were just plain cranky. Experienced guides told me the same thing—avoid bachelor buffalo at all costs. In a herd, the males offer protection to the group but have the backup of hundreds, even thousands, of their own kind. Understandably they feel secure in this situation and are less likely to trample you, or jab you with their pointed horns. Once aged, the males start to lag behind the group and are forced to live on their own. This tends to put them in a bad mood. Occasionally they form small clubs, but even these grumpy old bulls are likely to vent their insecurity on any slow-moving guide who crosses their path. Before moving to Botswana I'd held a secret belief that the reason guides claimed so much fear of buffalo was because if they were attacked by something, they wanted it to be a bit more glamorous than a glorified cow.

I was wrong.

Buffalo started to haunt my morning rounds as I went to wake up the guests. Our camp was built under the shade of ebony and leadwood trees, with the occasional thicket of woolly caper bush and date palm growing underneath—just the sort of location old buffalo like to hang out in. Twice in my first two weeks at Mombo Camp, buffalo charged off as I approached, and I started to wonder exactly how my position had become available—and where the last guy was buried.

Bleary-eyed one morning, with caffeine still missing from my system, I fumbled my way along the dusty path to the guest tents, calling out "Good morning!" in as cheery a voice as the hour would allow (it was barely after five o'clock, and the sun had only just cracked the horizon). I heard a rhythmic thumping, getting rapidly louder, and I turned to find 1,600 pounds of pissed-off cow bearing down on me. Clearly it disagreed with my assessment of the morning.

As much as it would make me feel tough and proud to say

that I stared it down or shamed it with a withering punch, I didn't. That doesn't work with buffalo anyway. They are never kind enough to mock charge and will always finish any attack they start. If a buffalo is running at you, you have to climb something or throw yourself flat and hope that the buffalo will miss and carry on running.

But there were no trees, or even termite mounds, around for me to scale, just one small acacia bush. And in my attempt to step backward, I tripped over my own feet, knocking the wind out of my lungs and landing deep in the shrub's thorny embrace. Never in my life had I been grateful for my disconcerting ability to trip on a level surface, but I was now. Never before had I thought that landing in a thornbush could be a good thing either, but again I did now as, wheezing, I watched the buffalo thunder over the spot where I had just been standing, then wheel back and snort. Where I had been before he could see nothing but the bush. And while buffalo can be credited with a degree of intelligence, this one did not possess enough to guess where I was unintentionally hiding. So he turned again and trampled off through the camp.

I tried to exit the bush with the same velocity that I had entered, tearing my flesh and quickly deducing that you can jump (or fall) into a thornbush, but you cannot jump back out. I took out the multi-tool that was attached to my belt and started clipping the branches that ensnared me until I could move without too much blood loss. I got halfway up, put my hands on my knees, and breathed. There was an absence of sound, until I stood up straighter, walked to the nearest tent, and shouted, "Good morning!"

Learning to Walk Again

In the South African reserve where my career started, I boldly carried a rifle on every walking safari that I led, despite having very little idea how to use it. I did know it was intended only for the most dire of emergencies, such as a serious charge from a lion, elephant, or rhino, but I couldn't imagine myself having the heart to actually shoot an animal—particularly because I often preferred them to the people I was leading. "Get up a tree," I once told a noisy family that had drawn the ire of a normally sedate broken horned rhinoceros. "I'll shoot you before I hurt him." And scramble up they did, with remarkable agility for such large people.

Because of this, the walks I led focused on dodging wildlife, not finding it. My aim was for my ineptitude with firearms to never be tested, nor the tree-climbing abilities of the tourists who were with me.

Despite this, the mere feel of steel in my arms became something of a security blanket, and once I had moved to Botswana and was told that I was to lead walks with nothing more deadly than a stick, I was quite anxious. "B . . . But, what if something charges us?" I stammered at Chris, who had explained to me that within a Botswana national park, no firearms were allowed, for any reason.

"You just have to make a plan," he said, as if that was the simplest thing to do when a large, fast, and deadly animal was bearing down on you and the tourists were most likely ignoring your directions not to run.

On my first walk, I clutched at the crooked stick that I carried as a surrogate weapon, explaining to the tourists about tracks, trees, birds, bees, and anything else that could be watched safely on foot. The tourists loved the walk and became excited that there was a world as fascinating, violent, and fast paced at the micro level as there was at the macro. I was just relaxing into my patter when I heard a sneeze.

It wasn't a human sneeze, but that of an impala. Impalas don't sneeze because of allergies, but as a warning that there is danger. Before I had time to explain this pertinent detail to the group, impalas started flying by us, kicking their legs high as they leapt.

Being new to the area, I was bemused by this almost dance-like stride. Later I would learn that the strange, rocking-horse run that they did was reserved for when they were being chased by wild dogs. It was designed to make it harder for the dogs to grab their stomachs and disembowel them. The lesson came quickly, as the dog pack was only seconds behind the impalas. And before I could explain to the terrified-looking guests that the tan, black, and white predators were no danger to man, we heard the death rasp of an antelope.

"No problem everybody," I said, clutching my stick. "We might head back to camp though now—that gurgle will attract other predators that are a bit nasty." There was no argument, only some sarcastic remarks about how I had explained at the start of the walk that the focus would not be on large animals.

Chris placated me on my return, saying it was a one-off incident. The next day I led another walk, and we bumped into a pride of lions. They politely backed away from us, perhaps wondering about the insane man that was pointing a stick at them as if it was something to be feared.

"This is ridiculous," I said to Chris, who was finding my run of "luck" very amusing.

"You could do what Old Joe used to do on his walks," he said.

"Which was . . . ?"

"Do you see that termite mound?" he asked. I couldn't miss it. From the deck of the camp it was one of the most prominent features, an edifice of clay that stood taller than two men and almost as wide as a Land Rover. I nodded to Chris that yes, I could see it.

"Joe would lead his guests to it, then sit them on the far side so they couldn't see how close they still were to camp. Then he'd take an hour telling of the time he was attacked by a lion, turn them around and walk them back. They loved it."

This to me was a travesty. Guiding was all about imparting your wisdom of the bush, making people aware of the value of all life, not just the lions and elephants, slyly trying to make conservationists of them while making the whole package entertaining. Besides which, I hadn't been attacked by a lion and doubted that people would sit still for an hour while I spoke of something as banal as my school days or growing up in the suburbs.

So on my next walk I trudged out again, sticking to the open plains, casting suspicious glances at every bush and termite mound, warily walking us far around groves of trees. The problem with this approach was that my knowledge of grass was limited, as was the tourists' interest in it. Perceiving their boredom, I begrudgingly trekked us through a narrow band of trees on our way back to camp, describing the animals that lived in it and how the group of trees came to be formed. We sampled some of the edible fruits, and to my most pesky guest I gave a tasty seedpod that causes hiccups. To get back to camp, we had one more plain to cross, then we needed to get through one last patch of low vegetation.

At the edge of the plain, a group of zebras were slowly making their way to the shade of the trees, but little else stirred. We moved forward, the group happy now that the camp was near and that they could soon have a cool drink. This is when accidents happen, the guiding books tell you, so I kept my guard up. When we were halfway across the plain, I was rewarded with a glimpse of an ominously shaking bush. There was no breeze, so it must be an animal causing the tremor, I thought to myself. I held my hand up and motioned for the group to stay silent.

A buffalo emerged from the bush with foliage draped over his horns, a ludicrous looking garland on such a cantankerous animal. For some reason the old boy was having a bad day. Many male animals when upset take out their frustration on inanimate objects, and this guy had just beaten up a bush. I had no doubt that despite being a vegetarian, he would be just as happy thrashing something meaty—like the group of us standing in the open plain.

With no breeze the buffalo wouldn't smell us, but seeing the group would not be a challenge. I made slow hand motions for everyone to squat, a prearranged gesture. I didn't look to see if they had followed my instructions. I just kept my eyes on the buffalo, waiting to see if he would spot us.

Click. Whir. Click. Whir.

I couldn't believe what I was hearing. But when I turned, my eyes confirmed what my ears had been telling me. One of the group, a young French honeymooner, was proudly standing with his little point-and-shoot camera and snapping photos of the buffalo as his wife tried to yank him down. The buffalo was now glaring at this new object with his yellow-ringed eyes. He stepped toward us, horns high and nose glistening.

I had no doubt that the bull was still cranky and would treat any target with the same rage as he had just displayed on the innocent bush. I wanted my rifle, mainly so I could shoot the French guy, but I knew that I had to do what Chris had said. I had to make a plan. There was no way we could make it back to the trees. I looked around the near-featureless plain, kicked the French guy in the shins, and waved for the whole group to follow me to a low termite mound. We hunched our way over to it, and I whispered for everybody to stay still and wait there for me. They had little shelter, and the buffalo was approaching rapidly now, so it wouldn't surprise me if they thought I was abandoning them. With no time for an explanation, I stood, ran sideways across the plain, and then swerved back into the group of trees we had come from.

I glanced over my shoulder to see that the buffalo had taken the bait. He was following the path I had run, head held high and nostrils flaring, at an angle that would take him past the tourists. Still, my plan was to get him right away from them, so I slunk further into the trees.

I had been deliberately flapping my sandals as I ran, to make sure I had the buffalo's full attention, but now I walked like Donald Duck, rolling on the edge of my feet to keep them quiet. I waddled the length of the grove, dropping to my hands and knees as I reached its fringe.

The zebras were still making their way to the shade, occasionally cropping at grass but mainly scanning their surroundings to make sure all was safe. They hadn't seen me in the shadows, so they were startled when I burst out, shouting and waving my arms at them. I ran in a loop from the trees, knowing they would rely on their speed to escape and not head for the trees, driving them toward the buffalo that was now very close to the termite mound where I had left my guests.

The zebras whistled as they ran, a surprisingly cheery sound for a call indicating danger. The buffalo knew exactly what it meant, as all the animals understand each other's words for danger. As the zebra herd reached him, he had a decision to make. Stay and face whatever was chasing the zebra, or take the safe option and run. I imagine his primitive and sinister brain weighing up his options, then coming up with the answer.

Bugger it, he would have thought, or some bovine equivalent, and he galloped off with the equids in a cloud of dust.

I collected the group, and we walked back to the camp in near silence—the only sound the swish of our feet and the occasional smack on the head the Frenchman received from his new wife.

I was quietly proud of my plan and how well it had worked, accepting the pats on the back from my guests. I felt that I could face whatever challenge the wildlife of Botswana threw at me, and that I had learned how to walk safely.

Nevertheless, on my next walk, and most of them afterward,

I walked a short way, sat my guests down on the enormous termite mound, and told them about the time a buffalo had almost caught my guests and me.

Princesses and Jacks

A specialist guide is someone who has been around long enough that he or she can market a safari to past clients and their associates, and on that alone stay busy and profitable. Some have a specialty to go with their name, like in-depth knowledge of birds or the night sky. The good ones tell stories that enthrall their clients at night around the campfire, and may even have an element of truth to them.

Before I ever became one myself, a specialist guide came to Mombo, and I learned that what I feared most was not getting killed myself, but having it happen to someone in my care.

This specialist was one of the good ones and was known to be a tad wild. His party included a couple who were members of the British royal family. They were far enough from the throne that it would take an extraordinary series of accidents for them to become king and queen, but they were close enough to it that they spoke with their teeth clenched, smelled rich, and somehow made you feel like Oliver Twist asking for more every time they spoke to you.

With them were their three grown children and another young guy who was friends with one of the younger royals. It was hard to tell which one, because at some point the mother must have given birth like a machine gun—Pop! Pop! Pop! They weren't triplets, but they did all seem to be around twenty. So did their friend, whose name was Charlie, and he too was a young lord or baronet himself.

It may have been Charlie who started it, but the commencement of that evening's festivities, like much of that night, is hazy. The guides often ended up in one of their or the manager's tents after all the guests had gone to bed. We'd play stupid drinking games or just drink. It relieves the strain of being polite all the time. Because these royals were young, and wanted to have fun, they got themselves invited to the rarely seen back of camp. In addition, the girl was pretty, and one of the guides had a bit of a thing for her already. "Guys," Hayden said earnestly. "I really like her. I think she likes me. Can you watch us and let me know if she likes me?"

"It's unlikely," said Al.

"You're not that good looking," added Anna, the English manager.

"Not that charming either," offered Robyn, the Canadian.

"Like an incontinent warthog," I finished.

This was the way we spoke to each other most of the time, in short offensive blasts. When we spoke to the young royals, however, we portrayed him as if he was some sort of god. Perhaps we were going too far, but we decided there was no point underdoing it and calling him a king, because this girl wouldn't be impressed by that. We needed to talk him up and hope that a lot of alcohol might make him more appealing.

There was solidarity in our effort. Most of the people that came on safari were too old or too recently married to be open to the seductive charms that a khaki uniform holds. If an attractive, single girl did arrive in camp, and there was a guy who didn't have a partner on the staff, we'd all do our best to help him. Otherwise you had to listen to them complaining about it.

That night there were three guides and two camp managers, plus the four young royals in the canvas-and-pole structure that we called a house. In Northern Botswana this is considered a large gathering. Al, the specialist guide, brought some poker dice that had the faces of various cards instead of numbers on them, and he suggested playing strip poker. None of us knew how to play poker, or how to use these particular dice, so Al suggested that we take turns rolling the dice and every time the jack's face came up, whoever had thrown it would take off an article of clothing or drink a shot of tequila.

For some reason it seemed like a good idea. Al was the only one in the room over twenty-five. We all started drinking, and then when we felt couldn't drink anymore, started stripping. On occasion somebody would wander off to the bathroom or outside to pee. (Outside was just as easy and private for the guys. The bathroom was only a basic basin and toilet screened by a thin sheet of canvas.) If you timed your exit right, you could avoid a turn with the dice and the chance of another tequila or lost garment.

Arguments as to whether a belt was clothing or not, and whether one sock counted, came and went, with a lot of joviality and drink pouring. Charlie, wearing only his underpants, got up and went out the door for a piss like most of the guys had been doing. We drank on and stripped down.

The noise we were making was just enough to drown out the usual night sounds of distant lions, shuffling porcupines, wailing bush babies, and the occasional alarm of an antelope that would make us all think "Leopard!" But we weren't too loud. If we became too raucous, we would keep the other guests awake and then have to deal with complaints from our bosses in the distant town in the weeks to come. We were professional enough to hush anyone who got too vocal, but not enough that we ended the game when we should have.

Finally Hayden was naked and pale in the lantern light. Nobody was sure if the game was over, because we were making up the rules as we went along.

It was decided that from that point on, if Hayden threw a jack he would have to fulfill a challenge, or down a tequila shot. At this stage the mention of the Mexican liquor was enough to make us all gag, but we were still having fun. Hayden announced that the game would be over only when everybody was naked. Al kept rolling queens and kings, and to this day I suspect him of cheating without a theory as to how, and soon he was the last one with a stitch on.

We all sat with our knees clutched against our chests for the little privacy it offered, but on occasion one of the girls would laugh a little too loud or readjust and you could sneak a peek. Maybe they were doing the same with us guys, but I don't think so.

Hayden had edged closer to the little princess and slithered an arm over her shoulders. We were all grinning at this with the subtlety of baboons, except her brothers, who didn't seem that happy. Then Hayden rolled a jack, the first fully naked person to do so. It was suggested that he make the sound of a dying warthog while standing naked in the clearing outside to see if lions would come, which the young princes liked the sound of, but Al and I vetoed it as too risky. Instead we made him do a flaming arsehole. This sophisticated challenge involves clenching five squares of toilet paper (or bog roll as it is known in Botswana) between the backside cheeks. These are then set alight, and an arbitrarily determined distance must be run by the individual. The heat encroaches and singes some places, and running barefoot is awkward over the thorny ground. But Hayden managed his challenge capably, and we all went back inside to carry on with the game. Hayden circled like a hyena trying to figure out how to get his arm around the girl again.

Then one of her brother's said, "Where's Charlie?"

I had never gone from dead drunk to stone-cold sober before. It is a sensation like an electric shock that leaves you tingling, alert, and with the taste of copper in your mouth. One minute your balance is off, you are laughing too much and too loud, and breasts seem to be the most magnificent things you have ever seen. Then you come back into sharp focus. You can see the imperfections, and the only remnant of drunkenness is the feeling of being a little sick.

I looked at Al, and his tan had disappeared. Hayden, Al, and I all grabbed our shorts at once and pulled them on. One of the disadvantages we had had in the game was that most safari guides don't wear underpants. It was an advantage though now because we were all dressed by local standards as soon as the shorts were on. Add shoes, and you're ready to go on a rescue mission.

We paused at the door of the house, sober enough to want a plan. Al took charge.

"Hayden, he's staying in tent 6, see if he made it back. Pete, head round to the main building."

We got the two managers to stay with the remaining royals and made some half-hearted reassurances that we were sure he would be okay, that he probably just snuck away to bed. I don't know exactly what the others were thinking, but my thought process went like this: Not lions. We would have heard them. Or hyenas. We would have heard them too—and if it were a single hyena it wouldn't have had the balls to jump him, even if he was staggering drunk. Maybe a leopard? But the leopards that we used to see were unusual, almost freakish, in their lack of aggression. Maybe, I thought, a single lion. Some female that had split from the pride to have cubs. She would do it with minimal noise and fuss to avoid hyenas. Shit.

As I walked with a flashlight that I didn't remember picking up, I suddenly started feeling very vulnerable and wished I had underpants on. It wasn't cold, but I felt a chill as the beam swung left, right, left, looking for the forward facing eyes of a predator.

"Charlie!" I hissed, still not prepared to wake the other guests. It would be morning until we could properly look for tracks to see which way he had gone and what had got him, but we all wanted an answer now.

Only now that I was away from the others did all the night noises crash back in. Owls hooted, screeched, or lewdly whistled, depending on the species. Toads croaked in the puddle made where we washed our cars. Somewhere, not far, a hyena whooped, and the hairs on the back of my neck grew bristly and stiff. The light arced around, and there was Al, coming around a corner of the kitchen tent. Both of our lights jumped.

"Fuck!"

"Shit!"

"Luck?"

"No."

"Bugger."

"Yeah."

We stood quiet for a moment, taking stock and pondering our careers. Among the mixed sounds of a branch scratching at the thatch and the animals calling, fighting, and dying, was a repetitive and unknown noise. It repeated at odd intervals, almost rhythmic but not quite. Guides follow new sounds, because they may lead to something they haven't seen before.

Al and I looked at each other, still breathing heavily, and wordlessly homed in on the sound. It wasn't far from the kitchen tent, maybe by the laundry room, but the noise was definitely organic. The generator had been switched off long ago, and you could tell when a sound was made by an animal. Every now and then Al and I would pause, shining our lights around and whispering Charlie's name. The sound never paused. It just kept its erratic beat.

Tap tap. Growl.

Tap tap. Growl.

It didn't sound like something feeding. That's a wet sound, with tearing noises mixed in. This was dry and raspy.

Tap tap. Growl.

We rounded the locked laundry door, and there sprawled against the wall, with his legs splayed in front of him, was Charlie. As our light played over his incongruously white underpants, he clapped weakly twice and gave out a hoarse "Hey!" in a scratched and vulnerable voice, just as he must have been doing for hours.

"Fuck," said Al.

"Yeah," I said.

"Hey," said Charlie.

After we'd carried him to his room, we went back and collected the royals, clothed now and looking young and awkward. We told them that Charlie had been found and was fine. He'd confessed that he'd wanted to sneak away, and thought he'd find his tent. He'd found some startled Belgians instead, backed away from their tent, and staggered off into the bush. Looking at his tracks the next day, it could only be considered a miracle that he'd made it back into the camp, such a wandering and tortuous path had he walked. When he'd found the laundry structure, he'd felt saved and was convinced his clapping and "heying" would keep any predators at bay for the rest of the night.

We escorted the guests (their status as guests had been restored with their clothes) back to their tents, bidding them all a safe good night, and regathered at the staff house. We did a half-hearted clean up, sweeping empty bottles into a bag and collecting the random and discarded clothes that still littered the floor. We all decided that the night was over, and shaken but relieved we started heading for our tents. There was only one unresolved issue.

"So," Hayden asked us as we moved into the darkness. "Do you think she likes me?"

You never knew what might be hiding inside the low clumps of palms that grew by the riverbeds.

Titus was studying to be a witch doctor, specializing in poisons and potions that he would often test on anyone foolish enough to let him. Like me. After willingly imbibing many of his concoctions with some startling results, I had to insist he give me nothing before a safari that would make me hallucinate or urgently need the bathroom.

I used to think guides were only afraid of buffalo because they didn't want the shame of being killed by a glorified cow. Then one chased me, then another, and another, and I decided that they really were quite frightening.

The aim of a safari walk (at least the ones I led) was to avoid large animals and to concentrate on plants and tracks. At Mombo this proved impossible, as on my first few walks, wild dogs, lions, zebra, and a particularly cranky buffalo convinced me that I should have taken up accounting.

Warthogs often munched the lawns surrounding Mombo during the day and were very relaxed around humans. This gentleman, however, took offense when I photographed his girlfriend, and he chased me up a tree. My coworkers found this very amusing. I did not.

CHRIS GREATHEAD

With hippos on either side of the car, it should have been obvious that I had driven too far.

While the two young female lions searched for their mother, she was canoodling behind my tent with one of the male lions from the north. Though this negligent behavior would not have won her awards as mother of the year, the real problem was that her indiscretion led to a territorial war between the two ruling lion factions of north and south Mombo. The chase that ensued was truly a once-in-a-lifetime event to witness.

Though I fought it as hard as I could, the beauty and abundance of the birds in the Okavango Delta (like this lilac breasted roller) won me over. After I found myself taking time to identify each species and ticking off a list, I had to admit that I truly was one of "those people"—a bird nerd.

Top: *Glancing around and hoping to spot predators rarely bears fruit, as they are very good at hiding. It's easier to rely on the sharper senses of other animals, such as these kudu. A group of animals staring in the same direction is a good sign that they have seen something distressing (in this case, a distant lion).*

Bottom: *As experienced safari guides, Cliffy, Paul, and I should have been able to find our way through the myriad twisting and plaited channels of the Okavango Delta. Instead, we spent four days in a wilderness that perhaps nobody had ever been to before, enjoying the best sort of adventure—an unplanned one.*

The estimable Rantaung Rantaung gave me the nickname Lehututu (or ground hornbill) as a reference to my unusual and somewhat comical tanning patterns. Although I shouldn't have, I became quite fond of the name.

Oryx were one of the few animals that could survive in the salt pans of the Madgkadigkadi, but other, more dangerous creatures—voracious mosquitoes and wandering donkeys among them—bothered me the night I was stranded there.

Two photographers, the other guides, and I spent months getting this family of cheetahs relaxed enough so that we could safely approach them. Still, Nick opted to take this photo from the safety of the Land Rover, all the while waiting for me to get eaten.

"Spielberg" was desperate for a photo like this. Unfortunately, the giraffe and bum-flashing zebras weren't as good at taking stage direction as he'd have liked.

Swimming among a herd of elephants gave me an unusual perspective for photography but must rate as one of the more foolish things I have ever done. Fortunately, this herd was led by Salvador, a regal elephant who tolerated my intrusion.

Although pythons kill by strangling, their curved teeth and the overwhelming stench of their feces can be just as bad—a lesson I learned the hard way when I attempted to move one.

The Okavango supports diverse habitats such as wetlands, dry plains, acacia woodland, riverine forest, and swaths of waving red grass, as could be found in an area we called "The Wheatfield." I loved driving here, hearing the swish of the tough grass blades against the vehicle and watching the occasional buttonquail flush from the grass and whirr away on stubby wings.

When an elephant charges, the position of its trunk should be noted. In a mock charge the trunk will be held loosely, not tucked safely away. This fellow is mock charging, but knowing that doesn't make ten thousand pounds of upset pachyderm running at you any less terrifying.

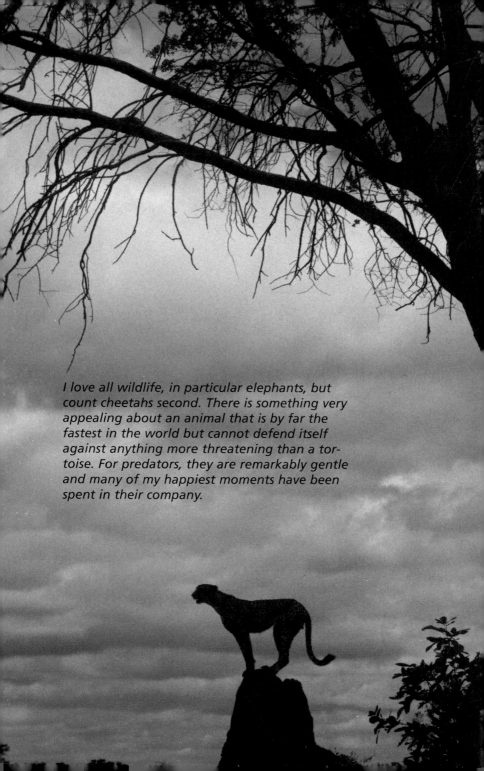

I love all wildlife, in particular elephants, but count cheetahs second. There is something very appealing about an animal that is by far the fastest in the world but cannot defend itself against anything more threatening than a tortoise. For predators, they are remarkably gentle and many of my happiest moments have been spent in their company.

Pets

Attie gave Yolanda a baby squirrel.

He claimed to have found it lying at the base of a tree, but we all suspected that he had stolen it from a nest.

Grant, Yolanda's husband, wasn't happy.

"Bloody Attie! You know what's going to happen, don't you?" he asked me. "She'll get attached to it, then something will kill it, and I'll be left to pick up the pieces."

"And if the Wildlife Department pays a visit and sees your wife with a pet squirrel, they'll arrest her," I added, just to cheer him up. It is illegal to have any animal in a national park. Even if Attie *had* found the squirrel lying naked and helpless at the foot of a tree, the law said he had to leave it there for the jackals to deal with.

Every single one of us at Mombo worked in the bush because we loved animals, and most of us missed the pets we'd had as children. So illegal or not, we couldn't just leave the baby to die. We kept the squirrel and named him Chap.

Prior to Chap's arrival, the closest thing to pets we had were a family of warthogs that spent most of their day in the camp. They were moderately tolerant of people walking close by, giving a gruff snort if you stepped too close to their grazing. They showed no affection to us, which is probably because we strictly adhered to the commonsense rule of not feeding wild animals.

There were other animals that had territories that included the camp and surrounds, and these would often allow close approaches without ever being anything like tame. The most relaxed were a small herd of kudu (a type of antelope), a baboon troop that visited every few days, a huge monitor lizard, and a group of naughty monkeys that came into the camp every day.

The monkeys were a problem. Unlike the warthogs, which seemed content with their lot and were unwilling to launch raids against the bounty held in our storerooms, the monkeys were constantly plotting and scheming ways of getting to our food. In the afternoon just before the game drive, guards would be posted around the afternoon tea as it was being set up to protect against the furry bandits. The monkeys learned distraction techniques and would have dummy runners scoot by to draw the attention of any watchers, as another shimmied down a tree to make off with whatever muffins or cakes might be set out. They even learned how to unzip tents, and took great delight in strewing the contents of unwary tourists' luggage around the bush, festooning the thorn trees with underwear like it was an early Christmas. They also had a sideline interest in shiny objects, which could keep them entertained for hours. People would often have the startling experience of going into their bathrooms only to find a monkey on the basin, admiring its reflection in the mirror.

The various managers who handled the food and beverages at Mombo Camp always ended up hating monkeys because of their theft. I also had a battle with them, but it was for a different reason.

Sleep is a sacred commodity to a safari guide. I started work at five o'clock in the morning and was on duty until after brunch at around eleven o'clock. In between then and three o'clock, I might have as many as three forty-minute round trips to the airstrip, and if I sat with the guests for dinner, my evening could run as late as midnight. This was the routine for seven days a week, three months straight. From about the midway point of any three-month stint in the bush I would be exhausted. And on the rare days that I had no guests to pick up or drop off at the airstrip, I would rush to my baking hot tent, soak a bedsheet, lie underneath its cool moisture, and try to doze for an hour or so. The monkeys seemed to want me awake, though, and took great delight in climbing the tree nearest to my abode and launching themselves at its taut canvas roof.

My "house" was just four poles stuck in the ground, with canvas wrapped around it and zippers front and back. One side was higher than the other, and the roof was yet another swathe of canvas that sloped down to allow runoff in the rainy season. To the monkeys' great delight, all that tight material had created an enormous drum, and they had a knack of landing on it just as I had reached a relaxed enough state to have a little drool going. The thud would be accompanied by a drum roll that would make a sergeant major proud, as four feet would scamper back to the edge of the roof, only to leap across to the nearest tree, climb it, and repeat the process.

If I rushed out of my house to bellow at them, I would gain no satisfaction, just a number of furry, gray-fringed faces that seemed to be laughing at me. Some would even call out "Kwo! Kwo!" as if to show how funny they thought I was, or maybe to point out the silver trail on my chin. As soon as I went back inside, they would start bouncing on the roof again. "Boom! Ga-doom, ga-doom, ga-doom, ga-doom," went the sound, and there was no way I could convince myself it was a lullaby.

Staggering out of my tent one day, bleary-eyed, bitter mouthed, and frustrated to the point of tears at the antics of the Botswana Trampoline Team (as I had come to think of them), I picked up a stick and threw it at one of them. It missed, but one of them said "Kwe!" I froze. He hadn't said, "Kwo!"

This was important.

I understand a little bit of monkey language, and "kwe" is a sound I listened for. It was an alarm. If I heard it on a drive, I would hone in its origin, see in which direction the monkeys were looking, and locate whatever predator it was that was disturbing them. If they were mildly panicked, it was usually only a snake; larger panic was for a lion or cheetah. Full-blown conniptions were reserved for leopards, because they could climb trees. The stick I had thrown had been briefly misinterpreted by one of the monkeys as a snake, and it gave me an idea.

"I need to borrow this," I said to Yolanda, who was sitting in the office that adjoined the rather tacky little curio collection we sold to supplement the camp's income. I was clutching a fluffy toy and grabbed a small scarf as an afterthought. "And this," I added and ran out, probably confirming Yolanda's opinion that I had spent a bit too much time in the sun without a head covering.

I ran back to my house, where the monkeys were in full swing. They scampered into the branches at my approach, but didn't move too far away from their game. They just sat bobbing and swaying, adding an occasional "Kwo!" which I was convinced was laughter.

"Kwo yourself," I said, and from under the scarf whipped out the toy—a rather poor representation of a leopard, but it was enough to put the heebie-jeebies into the monkeys. They went berserk. "Kwe! Kwe kwe kwe kwe kwe! Kwe!" The whole troop had now moved away a few trees, but still watched the predator I held in my hand. I tossed it from side to side, and the pitch of their calls went up an octave. I was amazed at their gullibility, but took great pleasure in it and derived even more at their reaction when I threw the toy in the air. The whole troop called "Kwe!" in unison; one even fell off his branch. Then they fled, yelling a chorus of "Kwekwekwekwe!" as they went, and I imagined they were saying, "Holy crap! Did you see that? A flying leopard!"

I paid for the toy, and left it outside my room wedged into a tree branch whenever I had the opportunity for a nap. And every afternoon I made a point of bringing it back into my room, mindful that the bigger, stronger, smarter baboons would rip it apart if they came through the camp, as they had already done to numerous hats and shoes that I had left outside to air.

At night the warthogs, monkeys, and baboons all slept, and we faced new animals that lived with us but also weren't quite pets. The most innocuous were two porcupines that snuffled around, picking up whatever vegetable matter they could and giving us the occasional fright when we had mistaken them for a bush.

Then there were the hyenas. They would appear soon after dusk, slinking around the fringes of the camp and growing bolder as darkness increased. Finally, when backs were turned, they would make a dash for the kitchen or any unattended plate of food. The guests ate up on a raised deck, but the guides and managers sat at ground level on their nights off, and we often lost our dinners by going to the bar for a drink refill.

We also had a genet that spent the day sleeping in the rafters above the dining table. At night, when it woke up, if there were only a few people still at dinner, it would explore the tabletop as everyone rapturously watched its sinuous beauty. A genet is a long-bodied relative of the mongoose but has the markings of a leopard and an exquisite kittenlike face that is almost impossible to dislike.

Impossible, that is, until he eats the closest thing to a real pet that you have. The staff managed to feel animosity toward him when two weeks after Chap the squirrel came into our lives, the genet ate him.

So we went back to having only the genet and warthogs as "pets," and eventually forgave the former for his natural behavior. We would watch it climb onto the large dining table and search for scraps of food. Its lithe body would wind between the half-empty butter dishes and many wine glasses that littered the surface. The guests, and even the jaded guides, would sit enthralled as it delicately picked at the morsels left on the plates, pausing every now and then to scan its surrounds for larger predators that we knew would never dare approach with humans around.

Allowing this behavior bordered on illegal. For very sound reasons you are not allowed to feed wild animals. They can grow dependent on the junk that you give them and, in the case of animals like baboons, can become aggressive when they want a fix. We let the genet have its nibbles, though, as it was nothing but a snack before it began its real business of looking for any more squirrels we might have.

And it wasn't long before we had another. Attie (who must have spent a lot of time climbing trees) was back in camp to fix something or other and arrived in the office with yet another baby that he had "found." It was pink and almost hairless; its eyes were only dark smudges behind closed lids. Yolanda fell in love with it at first sight. He was quickly named after his deceased predecessor and became known as Chapter Two. The little bundle drank milk through an eyedropper until he became interested in fruit, nuts, and the decorations in the curio shop. To Yolanda's dismay, he gnawed at almost everything in the store with an insatiable appetite. Despite these problems, we all loved having him around. I spent up to ten hours a day watching animals, but nothing can compare to having fur to pat and innocent eyes that look at you with love. Perhaps I just needed a girlfriend, but I really fell for Two.

Chewing on things of value was not Two's biggest vice. He liked to hitchhike, and without any warning would launch himself from tree branches, thatched roofs, and the lightning conductor onto whoever might be walking by. The staff got used to these aerial assaults, but a visiting English lady became apoplectic when Two latched onto her leg as she stood at the breakfast buffet. She danced around, unsure as to what sort of creature was attacking her, panic written all over her face. Chapter Two clung on tighter still. Then when the woman stopped moving momentarily to clutch at her chest, Two scuttled to the safety of her head, which set her off again. Somehow, up to this point, the woman had held grimly onto the plate that she had been loading, but now she sent the eggs, cold cuts, and fruit flying. Chapter Two quickly launched himself after the bounty, contentedly chewing away as the camp managers and I attempted to calm his victim.

We took to warning guests about the resident attack squirrel when they first arrived in the camp, as part of the overall safety speech that we gave to everybody. If it were the first camp the tourists were visiting, they would listen intently as we detailed the actions required if they encountered lion, leopard, elephant, buffalo, or hippopotamus. Most would look bemused, though, at our description of the leaping squirrel after the other more deadly creatures, but they could no longer claim they weren't warned.

Once they had been alerted to his nature, the visitors usually fell for Chapter Two as well. He was an African tree squirrel, which is a much smaller species than those familiar to Americans or Europeans, but has the same cute features. People were even more charmed by him when he made an unlikely friend.

Two's buddy wasn't another squirrel, and its appearance was as much of a surprise as Two's sometimes was. At night Yolanda had started placing Two in a metal cupboard that sat outside the canvas-and-thatch office where she and the squirrel spent most of their time. Two had shredded some of the office paper and a bit of someone's cap to make himself a nest, and it was obviously cozy enough to attract company. One morning when Yolanda was opening the cupboard that she kept locked against the genet, Two jumped out, followed closely by a mouse. They tumbled together on the ground for a moment, apparently in play, then the mouse darted into the grass and Chapter Two ran up Yolanda's leg to say good morning. It became a routine and even reached the point that the mouse would be waiting outside the cupboard as dusk fell, nervously scanning the sky for aerial predators.

The mouse was as wild an animal as the warthogs, baboons, kudu, and monkeys that visited the camp, and never let us touch it. We grew enormously fond of it, though, and loved that Two had a playmate closer to his own size than we were.

One morning, though, neither of them exited when the door was unlocked. The day before, one of the camp hands had dented the metal door, raising the corner of it just enough for a predator to slip in. Maybe it was a snake, maybe the genet. We would never know.

"No more pets!" Grant declared, because as he had predicted with the very first squirrel, Yolanda was distraught. We all were, but the guys felt the need to make light of it. At breakfast we would point at the furry, banded tail that hung from between two rafters and address its owner, the genet, "Did you eat Chapter Two? Come down here so I can smell your breath. If it smells like our squirrel, I'm putting you in an omelet."

The genet ignored us, as did any animal that you spoke to. Yolanda would never forgive him and made sure she had left the table before he ventured onto it after dinner. Once again, though, his irresistible beauty bewitched the rest of us, and we would sit as quietly as the mouse he probably ate while he swirled amongst the wreckage of our dinner.

One evening, a few months after the demise of Chapter Two, there was a small group of clients at the table, plus Grant and me. The genet was making its way on the table, delicately sniffing at the scraps. One of the guests said, "Oh look, here comes another one."

Grant and I shot blank looks at each other, then reeled as a squat black-and-white animal the size and shape of a wolverine hauled himself onto the table and growled at the world. It was a honey badger, a creature that tourists don't hold in the same esteem as many of Africa's glamour animals, but guides do. It has a reputation for being unafraid of anything, indestructible, and ferocious.

"Shit!" Grant said, breaking the managerial protocol and swearing in front of guests. The lapse was justifiable.

"Everyone," I swallowed, "slowly, and quietly, push your chairs back from the table."

The genet hadn't bothered with slowly or quietly, and in its hurry to get off the table had knocked over a small milk jug. The badger did a shuffling trot over to it and began to noisily slurp at the puddle, pausing every now and then to show off its milk moustache as it growled at us—just to let us know we shouldn't think of taking its bounty.

Grant and I got the guests off the deck and safely to bed, suppressing the sort of hysterical giggles that come even to tough bushmen when a crisis has been narrowly averted.

"Bloody hell!" I said, as we stood at the side of the deck and watched the animal plow face-first into another plate of leftovers. "Where'd he come from?" Honey badgers aren't endangered, but you don't see them often at all—and no animal is ever as bold as this one was on its first encounter with humans. It must have been lurking around the camp unseen for weeks before deciding we weren't dangerous and that it was time for it to take over.

We soon realized that the honey badger was there to stay. He started arriving almost every night, to the terror of the kitchen staff. There are many African superstitions that surround the honey badger, as there should be for what must be one of the planet's toughest animals.

Honey badgers belong to a group of only four animals that

lions tend to avoid. The other three members are elephants, rhinoceroses, and hippos. The last three are all enormous with tough skin and armed with weapons like tusks, horns, or massive teeth. The badger is only about two feet long and built low to the ground. It is not fast and has no venom.

What it does have is tough but baggy skin that helps protect the animal against bee stings. The bagginess also allows it to twist almost 180 degrees if grabbed. If an animal is foolish enough to get a hold of a honey badger (and young lions and leopards sometimes try it—but only once), it faces two nasty defensive strategies. The first is an odor that the badger releases from its anal glands. Its stench would make a skunk ashamed of itself. The other is disproportionately long claws. When attacked, the badger aims these claws at the genitals. Anything bleeds to death very quickly if slashed in this area, and the badger has killed animals as large as buffalo that have done something to upset it.

So it was a mixture of fascination and crossed-leg trepidation that we lived with the badger as a nighttime visitor to the camp. As if he were a tourism veteran, he soon tired of the front of camp and only came to the back, where the staff lived and worked. He would raid the kitchen at will, arriving just after dusk. We had spent considerable time and energy hyena-proofing the kitchen building, which was a flimsy structure of canvas and eucalyptus poles. Thorny branches surrounded the building to a height and depth that normal animals couldn't penetrate. The badger just put his head down and, seemingly oblivious to the pin-sharp and inch-long acacia thorns, plowed in, slashed an entrance through the canvas, walked straight to the garbage bin, hooked his back legs over its rim, and bungee jumped in. At first the native staff would squeal and climb onto the benches, but soon they grew used to Badge, as we named him, and carried on with their business, stepping around him as they needed to.

Badge would emerge from his forays into the garbage with a mucky face, lick his paws, and settle by the dented and rusty trestle table where the guides and managers ate their dinner when not with the guests. It was somewhat unnerving trying to eat a meal with one of Africa's most ferocious animals sitting only a foot away from us. But Badge would calmly watch us eat, making a surprisingly cute twittering sound every time one of us lifted food to our mouths. As the meal wore on, growls would be interspersed with the twittering, until the whole experience became unsettling enough that whoever was closest to Badge would break the rules of our company, the ethics of our profession, and the law of Botswana by flinging him something to eat. As soon as the treat hit the bare earth, he would jump onto it, voraciously chomping through whatever bone and gristle it contained (we were never fed as well as the guests). As he finished, his face would settle into what looked very much like a grin.

A honey badger's face isn't as pointy as its European's namesake, and is therefore a little more humanlike. The silver on its back extends only as far as its forehead, making it appear to have a short fringe. If you ignore the claws and mutilating tendencies, you could even call the animal cute. Despite my reservations and the distance I kept, I started to like him.

When Badge sat beside me at the table, making his oddly birdlike noises and looking at me with his little dark eyes, it was easy to start thinking of him as a pet. None of us ever had the courage to pat him, though, and I've never seen as many guys sit through whole meals with their legs so firmly crossed.

■ ■

As unusual as his arrival was, it wasn't long before Badge wasn't even a novelty, and having him follow us around was as normal as walking an unleashed dog. We knew he wasn't dependent on the camp for food, because sometimes he would disappear for days, even weeks at a time. We would grow concerned that something had happened to him, until he would nonchalantly reappear, tear a hole in the kitchen wall, and jump in the bin.

We never saw Badge during the day. He may have been sleeping, he may have been foraging elsewhere; there was so little research available on honey badgers at this point that we really didn't know what he might be up to. But most evenings, just as the guests sat down to dinner, he would appear, have his meal from the bins, then sit by the table with the staff. On rare occasions, if someone got up, he would follow them a distance, but he would lose interest quickly and go back to his mixture of begging and threatening to those who were still eating.

One night he followed me farther, but at first I didn't realize it. The walk to my little canvas house took less than a minute in daylight, but at night I took it more slowly, scanning the surrounds with a flashlight in case there was something in the path. It had become enough of a ritual that I was probably a bit too relaxed when I heard a growl.

For reasons I've never understood, I am incapable of telling what direction sound comes from, so I swung the flashlight around wildly, looking for the owner of the threatening voice.

It was Badge. He was a few feet behind me, the short silver hair on his back erect, all paws firmly planted, and his mean glare directed at a point that I now had my back to. Anybody who has owned a dog or cat has had this done to him or her. It is freaky in an empty room, but in the pitch-black bushland, where the threats are very real, it is downright terrifying.

"What is it, Badge?" I asked, knowing how much I must have sounded like the kid from Lassie.

He growled again and stamped one of his feet, sending a puff of dust toward the adversary that I couldn't see, even though I was shining my light in the direction he was staring.

"You're not just messing with me, are you, Badge?" I've never felt foolish talking to animals, but I do think it is ridiculous to expect a reply. Badge, though, seemed determined to communicate that there was danger, and his erect tail started shifting from side to side, like a cobra shaping up to strike.

"Oh please don't fart."

The odor that came was so powerful that my eyes still water thinking about it. It filled the air like a blanket, cloying and noxious. Nothing I had ever faced in the bush had given me such a strong urge to run, but I was sure that whatever Badge was protecting me from would chase me if I did. I jabbed the light around, desperately looking for the telltale eye shine. None came. Fearing Badge's excretions more than any predator, I charged in the direction he was staring, and Badge gave a little "huff" noise as if to say, "Damn fool! That's where the danger is!" I wasn't sure if he was backing me up or not, but I figured that being eaten was a faster death than being suffocated.

I was moving the light around fast enough now that it would disturb the predator if I was lucky enough for it to be epileptic, but I still couldn't see what Badge was trying to gas. In a wild sweep, on the edge of the light, I caught a flash of—fur—tawny fur. I swung the light straight back and shone it full-on the stuffed leopard that I had forgotten to bring inside that day.

Badge growled at it.

That night I couldn't sleep. I wondered if Badge actually cared about me like a dog does its master, or whether he thought of me as one of his young. The main reason for my insomnia, though, was that no matter how many times I had washed myself, I still had an unholy reek emanating from my pores.

■ ■

Badge kept visiting the staff, and was always hesitatingly welcomed. He was the only truly wild animal I knew that ever became a pet, or decided that we were his. Eventually a new camp was built at Mombo, and the old one was torn down. The sites were only a few hundred yards apart, and we all expected Badge to turn up one day, flip the lid off a bin, growl, and make us laugh nervously again as we covered our most delicate parts. But he never did, and I never saw him again.

The Drowning

On safari you find that nature has a rhythm, an organized pattern of activity. There is a peak in the morning, as the nocturnal animals hurry through the last of their business and the diurnal species wake up, stretch, and start sniffing around for food and danger. As midday approaches there is a lull, as most living things go dormant in the heat of the day. When the afternoon cools there is a reawakening, as the animals shed the listlessness that the heat had cloaked them with. At night there is even more happening, but most of it remains unseen in the darkness. Like most camps we took advantage of the coolest parts of the day to do our safari drives, one starting in the afternoon at four and the other in the morning at the rather rude hour of five.

In the mornings, I was always in a hurry to get out into the bush. Many of the guests were startled to be woken so early, particularly as they were on holiday. The shock was doubled by my haranguing them to move quickly. I would do it as gently as I could at first, then become more forceful as my frustration increased, reminding them that they could have muffins and coffee anywhere, but leopards were a rare sight and every moment spent dawdling was an opportunity lost to find one.

"Don't you ever get tired of doing this every day?" they'd ask, sometimes a little exasperated.

"Tired, yes. But never of watching animals."

Sometimes people would ask me to expand. I think this was a stalling tactic so they could finish their muffin.

"When my alarm goes off, I hate it with a passion," I would explain. "Then I remember where I am, and that once I drag my backside out of bed I'm going to go and watch wild animals. If you had told me as a boy that this would be my job, I wouldn't have believed you. All I ever watched on television were nature documentaries and the occasional James Bond film. I thought that because they were on television they had the same degree of reality. So if you had asked if I wanted to be a safari guide when I grew up, I would have said no, because to me it was as foolish and unrealistic as wanting to be a debonair super-spy. So when I get really tired now and it's cold and my pillow feels too good to leave, I remember one thing: I've got the coolest job in the world. I'm James Bond. Now finish your muffin or I'll leave without you."

My cajoling sometimes bordered on harassment, but it meant that I was usually the first guide to leave the camp and the first to see what the animals were up to. I had four people with me that morning who had all arrived in camp the afternoon before. On their first drive they had seen plenty of herbivores and a small group of snoozing lions. I was hoping for a little more action on this drive. It was late winter and the air was crisp and still carried the nighttime scent of damp grass. The flood season was just ending in the Okavango, so the entire landscape was lush with greenery, dotted with small pools of water fed by dwindling channels.

Barely after we had left camp, two young male cheetahs

strolled across a short grassy plain in front of us. It required no skill to spot them, and as I was still sleepy, I offered a silent thank you to them for making my job so easy. We watched for a while, but they both had full bellies so were unlikely to do anything of great interest. It was only moments after we found them that they indicated their day's plan by flopping down on the side of a termite mound. I radioed their location to the other guides so they could have a look, and we moved on.

We drove for only a few more minutes, and rounding a corner we found a leopard climbing down a tree, right beside the road. While my guests were delighted, I was slightly irritated for two reasons. As a guide you want to pace things during somebody's stay. If they see everything at once, there will be too high an expectation on following drives. The second reason was that I had the skills to find these animals if they weren't being such exhibitionists, and I wouldn't have minded the opportunity to show off some tracking and wildlife-interpreting ability. Despite my disappointment, the two couples had both been on safari before and were staggered by our luck.

"We've never seen a leopard," the English couple gushed. "It's very exciting."

"We have, in Mala Mala," said Bob the American, naming a South African camp. "But not as close as this, and it wasn't as active." Mombo is blessed not only with an abundance of leopards but with animals that are very relaxed with the vehicles, having never been persecuted by hunters or large numbers of tourists, so they behave as if you aren't there at all. We watched this individual for a while until he too settled, and figuring the morning couldn't get any better, I proposed we stop for a coffee, a little earlier than we usually would. Beside me on the passenger seat sat a picnic basket with tea bags, instant coffee, thermoses of hot water, tightly sealed Tupperware containers of milk, jars of sugar, and home-baked cookies. Africa can be more civilized than people imagine.

We started driving toward a lagoon that was filled with hippos. It was a spectacularly scenic place to stretch your legs, and the receding floodwaters had left the surrounding areas dotted with wildflowers. Water lilies blossomed in the deeper parts of the channels that fed the hippo pool, and hundreds of storks, terns, herons, and skimmers preyed on the fish trapped in the shrinking ponds. The birds dipped, stabbed, and waded—a festival of color and movement. And as we drove through, they would lift up like balloons released at a carnival, settling again behind us.

I stopped to look at the tracks of a large herd of buffalo that had passed through the area. They were fresh enough for me to think the herd must have been there within the last half hour. I looked in the direction the spoor was heading, but I didn't see them. My eyes followed the tracks in the direction from which they had come, to see if maybe some of the herd was lagging. I thought about following the tracks, wondering if it was worth it after such a productive morning already. I had just settled on having the coffee instead when in the distance I saw a small group of birds fly up. They circled, and I could hear their harsh calls of alarm. I saw some antelope watching the area the birds were in, nervously stamping their legs.

"I think he's seen something," the American woman said to her husband, as if somehow I wouldn't hear her or like Lassie would thump my forepaw to indicate what it was that had my attention.

I didn't thump anything or say a word for a moment; I just kept watching. In a slight hollow I saw a glimmer of gold fur as a crouching figure slid forward. It was a lion, and it was stalking. It was turning into an incredible morning, but I was almost tempted not to point out the big cat. The group still had three more drives together, and after a morning of cheetah, leopard, and then lion everything would seem like an anticlimax. In the end I made my decision based on selfishness. The whole reason that I was in Africa was because I loved animals, and there was still nothing I enjoyed more than watching them.

"Lions," I admitted. They were a fair distance away from us, and I had only been able to spot them because the Okavango is so flat you can see for miles. With my binoculars I could see that it was a female with three young males. This was the second small-est pride in the area. As with most of the lions at Mombo, I could immediately recognize the family by its territory and the number and gender of its individuals. The males were the female's sons, too young to be a threat to the dominant males and not quite old enough to be useful hunters. They were about two years old, with the first wisps of mane surrounding their faces. Within the year, their father and uncle who ruled the entire north of Mombo would drive them away, before they could challenge them. Until then they would stick by their mother, who was their nurturer, provider, and often unwilling playmate as they roughhoused with her tail while she tried to catch food. In fact their only value was that they were fearsome looking enough to keep hyenas at bay when a kill was made. Their mother didn't have it easy.

"This pride is marginalized because it only has one adult," I explained to the guests. "Bigger prides with more adults don't want competitors around, and have pushed this little family into the flooded areas all winter. We see them hunting in the water quite often and have started calling them the Otter Pride."

As I spoke I was weighing which route to take to get a closer look, or whether to follow at all. The plain was muddy where it wasn't still under shallow water, and I knew there was a fair chance of getting the vehicle stuck. If I had known that getting bogged in the mud was not the worst thing that could happen, I would have held my tongue and not pointed out the lions at all. Instead I explained that we would do some real driving to get a little closer.

The lions were setting up to stalk a herd of antelope, so I didn't want to get too close and draw attention to the hunters. Instead I planned on looping around both predators and prey, so that when the chase occurred they would be running straight at us, which is a spectacular sight. The guests were enthusiastic about the plan, and at first I made encouraging progress. Across the plain were a number of low mounds made by a type of grass-eating termite. These created small islands, and I zigzagged from one to the next, racing across the sticky patches in between.

The lions kept moving, we kept following, and the water got deeper. First it was only midway up the tires, then it started sloshing over the running boards. Some started to seep through the decayed rubber seals of my door, making my feet cold. I had some small doubts about our ability to get any closer to the lions, but I was twenty-three years old and thought I was James Bond—so I pushed on.

By now there was a voice at the back of my mind that was nagging me, insisting that I just say to the guests, "Well, we can't get any closer. We've seen so much already. Let's go back and have our coffee, such a lovely morning, really," but I had a masculine imperviousness to nagging and was enjoying myself skidding around in the mud. I started to show off and was shouting out the names of the plants and birds we passed as we revved and roared through the deepening water. "Black-winged stilt! Wild date palm! Vlei ink flower! White-browed coucal! Water lily!"

Oh bugger, I thought. Water lilies only grow in deep water. Before I could impart this nugget of information, the vehicle plunged abruptly into a channel, dropping near vertically.

The hole we were in could only be a narrow channel, I thought, as there was a dense island of trees nearby that would grow only on higher ground. As a wave came over the bonnet and soaked me (the Land Rover had no roof, nor a windshield), I gunned the engine, which was now burbling strangely, and we shot up the opposite bank. I kept revving, and we slid onto firmer ground. I let the engine run until it had burped out whatever water it had swallowed. Then I switched it off.

As much as I disliked the thought of what my guests must look like, I turned around.

It was motley.

The couple from England was sitting on the rearmost of the three tiers of seats, which offers the best viewing but is also in the firing line of any mud that spits off the front wheels. It was apparent that while I was avoiding getting stuck by plowing on, they had been splattered several times. But instead of being the usual blotchy and spotted mudpack, they wore a streaky, Jackson Pollock–like mess. The wave of water had splashed them just enough to cause all the ooze to run down their rather bedraggled-looking clothing. The

Americans were not much better off. While they had avoided the worst of my mud flinging, the wave that had shot over me had landed full force on the first row of seats, where they were sitting. Their hair was plastered to their faces, and the lady had the leaf of some aquatic plant behind her ear. They looked rather grim, and reading their faces gave me the impression that they did not think highly of me or the way I drove.

"Well," I said. "I don't think we'll be going back that way."

That decision was as big a mistake as following the lions in the first place, which I now announced we would be giving up on. The cats had continued through the floodplains, and I knew that if we carried on it could only lead to us getting stuck so badly that I would have to call for help to get us out. And like all guides I hate having to call for help.

After some placatory language to my guests, and apologizing for their damp state of affairs, I announced that we were now on the other side of the very lagoon that I had intended to stop at earlier. The lagoon is fed by a channel in the opposite direction from the way in which we had come. I remembered when it had dried up the year before that there was a place in that channel where the bottom was sandy and shallow. We would cross there, have our coffee, and then make a slow way back to camp for breakfast, maybe finding the buffalo herd whose tracks we'd seen and, despite our aquatic incident, could still declare the morning a great success.

The Americans were resilient and gave a cheery thumbs-up, already over their soaking. I believe that Bob secretly wanted us to get stuck, because it would seem kinda manly. The English couple had gone very quiet, as if by saying nothing they wouldn't excite me and make me do anything else that was quite as dramatic as their submersion.

I drove along the edge of the lagoon, dredging my memory for some landscape detail where the shallow crossing had been. Following the lions had taken us far from any track, and it was only because I had spent up to ten hours every day for more than a year driving around the area that I had any idea where we were. As I looked I tried to remember the rule for using ripples to find shallow water, but I couldn't recall it. Then the song "Still Waters Run Deep" popped into my head. Excellent. The only problem was that the entire lagoon, floodplain, and channel were rippled from the breeze. Eventually I grew exasperated by the constant and uniformly striated expanse of water, and convinced that my faithful Land Rover could do almost anything, I said, "This is the place," and turned in to the water.

With trepidation I inched us forward, and to my pleasant surprise could feel by the way the car drove that we were on sand, not mud. This was good. Confident, I pushed on, and the waters rose over the running boards again. A hippo snorted in the lagoon to our right, and received a reply from another to our left. Must be another pool up there, I thought to myself. The water was now approaching the hood, my nerves were taut, and I handed the picnic basket with the coffee, tea, and cookies back to Bob just before the passenger seat that it had been resting on was submerged. My legs were next to go under, the water having easily pervaded the many cracks in the door, and the chill started reaching sensitive parts as it sloshed onto my seat, then above my waist. I knew that if forward momentum was maintained, the diesel engine would be fine, so stalling wasn't a problem. If the wheels slipped though, just once, we would be stuck.

"Are there alligators here in this water?" Bob asked.

"No," I said, concentrating on our momentum, willing the bottom to stay firm. "Only crocodiles."

I pushed a little harder on the accelerator to keep going, and we went a little faster. Our bow wave grew, as did my confidence, then we launched off the lip of a deeper channel that the hippos must have carved as they walked up and down from lagoon to lagoon.

We sank.

Water gushed in from all sides, over my door and the high sides of the vehicle. I grabbed at my handset as I watched the radio go under.

"Old Trails Hippo Pools! Old Trails Hippo Pools!" I shouted, giving our location in the hope someone might look for us, knowing I had maybe a fraction of a second before the radio died.

The engine cut out, dead along with any forward momentum. Waves radiated away, and hippos began snorting on both sides of us, as if they were laughing. Once again I looked over my shoulder. The American couple had shown remarkable agility for people of their size and scrambled back to the highest, rearmost seat, stuffing in with the English pair, who now looked terrified and quite cramped.

Never had I felt such fear. I had made mistakes before, but the results only endangered me. There was no way anyone would know where to start looking for us when we didn't appear for brunch, and the Mombo area covered three hundred thousand acres.

The vehicle was giving soft lurches, settling into the sand

beneath. Much more, and everyone would float off. As it was, only my head was above water.

I made a quick plan, but time was of the essence. "I've gotta go! The splash will have scared away any crocodiles! They'll be back soon to investigate! Gotta go before they do! I'll get back to camp and bring help!" I was not panicking, but was only a hair away from it, my words coming fast and breathlessly. I did not mention that of all animals, only the crocodile scares me, and it is a fear that runs deep and puts ice in my veins. "I'll be as fast as I can," I said. Then I added, probably unnecessarily, "Don't move."

I climbed onto the hood and slippery-dipped down into the water, splashing in and swimming as fast as I could. My sister had been a champion swimmer, but I had not. The stroke I use is high on energy and low on style and offers little propulsion even though I churn the water to foam. My arms whirred and my legs kicked furiously, but I seemed to be making little progress. I was sure that large, single-minded reptiles had to be closing in. I knew my theory about crocs being scared away by the splash of our vehicle was only fifty-fifty at best, and equal measures of fear and cold were making my bones ache. My winter clothes were slowing me and weighing me down. My kicks became more desultory, and my legs dangled. Then they touched something. The panic stirred me to whirr some more, until I realized that I hadn't put my feet on a croc.

It was the bottom. I quickly stood upright, wondering how long it had been reachable and feeling a bit silly. But I was still in danger, as a croc could easily drag me back into the deep, so I waded with ferocity, pushing a wave in front of me until I burst onto the shore.

While swimming was never my sport, I *had* received my mother's genes and was a runner. Now with the mantra of "Whatever you do, don't run" in my head, I ran.

With a final wave to the people on their odd-looking island that jutted out of the water, I cut across a plain, wanting to be able to see anything that was coming at me. It was later in the morning now, so I didn't expect lion or leopard to be particularly active, and daytime hunters like cheetah and wild dog are not really threatening. What did concern me was getting caught in the open by an elephant, buffalo, or, worse, a hippo heading back to the water after a night out foraging. More concerned for my guests than for myself, though, I ran on, scattering the plains game as I went.

Zebras and wildebeest gave alarms and raced away from the mad-looking figure that sprinted into their midst. A pair of warthogs showed the surprising speed their short legs can generate and startled me, bursting away from a low shrub. I kept running, getting tired. Good genes or not, the life of a guide is mainly sitting behind a steering wheel, and it had been years since I had run anywhere near this far. I had been going more than ten minutes at a pace much faster than a jog. I had a stitch, but kept lifting my legs and plonking them back down.

The plains of the Okavango are disrupted by islands of trees, often forming a perfect circle. Ahead of me was a possible shortcut back to the camp, which would cut a fair chunk out of the distance I needed to go. But if I cut through this patch of forest, it would take me out of the relative safety of the plains and through thicker, more concealing vegetation. I took the chance. Panting and feeling sick I ran up the small hump into the island and straight into the back of the buffalo herd whose tracks we had seen earlier. Some of the herd immediately bellowed and snorted.

Bugger, I thought, and ran straight back out, looping around the herd, forced back onto the plain. I skirted the edge of the trees I had just left, as the plain in this area was thick with small clumps of palms. These are one of the favorite resting places of old male buffalo, Africa's most foul-tempered animal. The odds of disturbing some cranky old buffalo that was in the process of being ejected from the herd was high, so I was now nervous of the herd to my left, unseen bulls to my right, and predators taking me from the front or back.

I ran in a way that would perplex an experienced jogger, swinging my head from side to side, looking to see if the herd was moving nearer to me or if a buffalo bull was emerging from the palms. Every now and then I would pivot entirely, checking behind to see if there was anything in pursuit. On one of these pivots, I saw some distant blonde heads pop up from the shade of a palm. They were the lions we had been following earlier. They must have doubled back to dry land, unsuccessful in their hunt. I watched them watch me as I ran, until one after another their heads went back down, clearly deciding I was not worth watching, or eating.

I put on a last spurt as I got closer to the camp, racing across the open area it looked out on.

In the ramshackle building we used as an office, Chloe said, "Is that Peter running toward us?"

"It looks like it," replied Ella. "I wonder where his guests are."

I burst in, breathless, trying with limited success to draw in great gulps of air. "Where," I gasped, "is Chris?"

"Where are your guests?" Ella asked, her English accent as always sounding to me like a scolding schoolteacher.

"Old Trails Hippo Pools," I said, feeling chastened. "I . . .," deep breath, "need Chris."

He was out back, and I ran there too, finding him in the workshop.

"I need two long chains, and two Land Rovers."

"Where are your guests?"

"Old Trails Hippo Pools," I repeated, "I need two chains and two Land Rovers." And oxygen, I thought, but knew I was in no position to start making jokes. Chris was an old friend and had shown a remarkable tolerance in the past when I had inconvenienced him. But he was still my boss, and there was no way that he could be pleased once he had seen what I had done.

We got in a spare vehicle and raced with chains to my stranded guests. "Where at Old Trails Hippo Pools are they?" Chris asked over the wind that whipped us and chilled the water in my clothing.

"The Pools."

"Ya, but East, West, where?"

"Just head to the Pools," I said.

■ ■

"Oh, I see," Chris said when we arrived. "In the Pools."

The four people huddled like shipwreck survivors on the only exposed parts of the vehicle looked absurd, but Chris wasn't laughing. I was in trouble.

"What . . . the fuck . . . were you thinking?"

I answered that I didn't think I had been thinking.

Chris bellowed across the water to the people to sit tight, we were going to make a plan. The English gent shouted back that he thought the car was slowly sinking, and we assured him we would make a plan quickly. They did appear a little lower in the water, but maybe I was only imagining it.

"What's the plan?" I asked, not sure if I should offer one or if I was so far in the doghouse that I should just shut up. Chris was South African, and South Africans pride themselves on making plans. In fact when presented with any problem, they say, "Don't worry. We'll make a plan."

What is never specified when they say this is whether you will like the plan, or whether after it has been implemented it will seem as sensible as when it was said. And since I was in no position to offer any sort of protest, I had to just watch as Chris tied one end of the chain to the front of the Land Rover we had arrived in and started wrapping me in the rest of its length.

"You go back out there," he said. "The chain will act as armor against crocs. If I see you go under because you've been grabbed, I'll just reverse and drag you out." I could see numerous flaws in this plan but kept them to myself. "It should be more than long enough," he added.

My clothes had dried on the run, but they were quickly soaked again as I plunged back into the lagoon. I had decided that while there was no way I could move faster than a crocodile, there was no point in namby-pamby creeping along either and moved as quickly as my ironclad limbs would allow. Progress was even slower than the time before, because my legs were exhausted and

I weighed almost twice as much as I had before. The sand and mud underfoot were sucking and holding me in place, and I thrashed with the last energy I had to keep moving. Every now and then my own exertions would plunge me down, and I grew sure that Chris would think I had been grabbed and would yank me out only for me to have to go back in again.

Halfway there, the chain pulled tight. "You've got to be kidding me!" I wailed to nobody in particular. The chain was long, but the bulk of it was wrapped around me, making it too short to reach the drowned car. I spun counterclockwise, releasing one of the coils around me and getting a pace closer to the submerged Land Rover. I turned again and again, shedding more of my armor, uncoiling the chain, and slowly making my way to the stranded vehicle. I was very conscious of the tasty-sounding splashes I must be making, just like an animal in distress.

Eventually I made it and dived under to blindly tie the chain to the grill guard. I scrambled back onto the hood and gave Chris the thumbs-up. Normally in a tow like this, I would sit at the wheel and steer, adding the stuck vehicle's engine power to the tower's, but our engine was dead. So I stayed perched like a hood ornament, too ashamed to speak much to the guests, beyond offering hope that we would get out quickly.

Chris started his engine and gave a few revs that echoed across the water. He started backing up, and we watched as the chain lifted along its length, then grew taut. At first there was no perceptible movement where I sat, just a slight vibration throughout the vehicle. I watched through the brown-tinged but transparent water as the grill guard started to peel away from the nose of the car.

"Whoa!" I shouted, jumping up and waving my arms, almost losing my footing. "Stop!" Chris was facing me, so he took his foot of the gas. There is nothing worse than having to shout that you have made a mistake, unless perhaps it is to shout that you have made another mistake. I hollered across the water to Chris that the bumper was coming off, and that I had to retie the chain. He didn't reply. He just waited for me to make a plan. I dived under again, in abject terror now because I was sure the activity must have aroused the curiosity of the water's denizens. Some hippos had, in fact, crept closer and periodically gave one of their trademark snorts as if to say, "Idiots!" Holding my breath and operating mainly by feel, I swam under the front of the car, finding the tow bar, tying onto it, and scrambling up onto the hood again. I gave Chris the thumbs-up, and still not speaking he revved his engine and reversed.

This time we came out with remarkable ease. There was a brief suck, then we surged forward through the water and onto dry land. It felt a little anticlimactic.

"You know," Chris said once he had pulled us far enough onto the plain to inspect the damage. "You weren't actually stuck. You drowned the car."

It didn't look that bad. The water had washed off almost all of the mud that had accumulated, and apart from the occasionally verdant patch of weed that was draped over the vehicle, it didn't look totaled. The grill guard was yanked at an angle that looked all wrong, but that was just a weld job, so I held out some hope for the vehicle.

The hope was misplaced. The engine had sucked up too much water to be worth repairing. I had just cost the company a lot of money. And to top it off, when the guests left they were asked to fill out an evaluation sheet. The Americans wrote an overall positive review. In the section asking about their guide, they gave me a rating of "good," and in their comments they simply wrote "Wild!" which could be read as good or bad. The English, however, no matter the attempts I had made for them to enjoy the rest of their stay (and the spectacular wildlife we saw before and after the drowning), still gave me a "poor" rating and wrote, "Too young. Needs driving lessons." You could almost hear them sniff.

It was rumored that the owner of the company read every single evaluation sheet. Up until then I knew that my reports had been positive. I was good at my job, I reassured myself. I knew a lot and delivered my knowledge with an obvious passion. What I wondered, though, was if this was outweighed in the eyes of my employers by the cost of a Land Rover.

Clearly it did, because I stayed on. Some months later the big boss did come to camp, and at one point he pulled me aside.

"You've been getting great reports. Well done." He scratched at his beard. "Some even sent in a photo of their stay. It showed a car underwater."

I didn't know what to say, so I let him speak next.

"Who do you think you are, James Bond?"

The Chase

The lions mated noisily behind my tent for most of the night. There was none of the awkwardness about this that you would expect if it had been, say, two of my coworkers, but their bouts at intervals of every fifteen minutes or so did make it hard to sleep. It was, therefore, with sleep-deprived crankiness that I greeted my guests the next morning and explained that we should be able to find lions easily. I slammed down an unhealthy volume of coffee and prodded my punters into the car. I was guiding a family of four and their escort, a woman from our office in Maun who had been sent to make sure that everything went smoothly, as the mother of the family was an important travel agent.

The lions had moved farther than I had expected. The tracks of the male were on top of the female's as she led him south, pausing every few hundred yards or so where there would be a patch of earth that showed (often quite pornographically) what they had paused for. I couldn't figure out why she would walk so far when mating, as lions rarely hunt while in the throes of passion.

Then I saw two lions, but not the ones I was looking for. They were young females, nervous and shy. As they walked they gave soft, mournful calls. "Awuuh," one would pant. "Awuuh," the other would add, the sound barely carrying. It's a call lions use when parted from their pride, and suddenly everything fell into place.

I knew this pride, I explained to my guests. We called them the Shy Girls. They were a beleaguered group of only three—a mother and her two girls—who were constantly being chased by larger prides from area to area but always in the south of Mombo. In the same region where the Shy Girls lived were two prides, each with at least three adult females and their young. The Shy Girls couldn't compete against them, so they just bounced around the south without being able to claim a territory of their own.

The Shy Girls' troubles were compounded by the difficulty of finding food. The two young girls were enthusiastic but unskillful helpers when their mother hunted. They often popped their heads above the grass to watch her stalk, sending her intended prey scattering. They reminded me of myself as a child, when I helped my mother shop by emptying whole displays into the cart.

If their mother was missing, I guessed it was because she was the female that I had been looking for that morning. And it would create quite a scandal in our lion community, because she was from the south and therefore shouldn't be with anyone except for one of the three absurdly blonde-maned brothers who ruled that area. We called these males the Beach Boys, but if she was this far north she had to be with one of the two brothers who ruled that part of Mombo. These two were big black-maned brutes.

Perhaps she had been driven north by one of the bigger southern prides just as she came into season, and the overpowering urge to mate drove her to briefly abandon her daughters. I imagined that she was now trying to get back to her comfort zone and the forlorn girls she had left behind. In the meantime her mate was going to make sure that no other male went near her while she was in estrus, and so he followed her south. If the Beach Boys caught him there with a female, a détente of many years would be shattered. War would break out.

I was excited, and I tried to transmit this to my guests, who nodded politely but showed as much enthusiasm as if I'd said we were going to have a knitting competition.

We watched the girls from afar, but they were upset, so I let them be and followed the tracks of their mother. Soon enough the track went through two low-growing bushes, before emerging into a natural amphitheater made by a ring of palms and riverine trees. In the middle was glaring-white sand and the lions we had been looking for, plus the second of the northern boys.

Clearly the female was now out of season, as the dominant of the two brothers was lying inelegantly on his back, legs splayed like a frog in a science project, exhausted after copulating about three hundred times in seventy hours.

The female was snarling at his brother, who was making a whining noise that robbed him of any dignity, and I imagined must mean, "Come on—three hundred times with him. Just once with me, please?"

But she was uninterested. And after about five minutes, I realized my guests were as well, so I decided to see what else was out and about that morning.

We emerged from the ring of trees to a beautiful plain covered in short grass like a golfing green, dotted with antelope and zebra. Straight away I saw that they were all facing the same direction. I sat higher in my seat to see what they were looking at, and in the distance saw three golden forms moving with a discernible purpose in our direction.

"Yes!" I exclaimed. "They're coming!" I was smiling wide enough to fit a fridge and swung around to beam at my guests, who just smiled back as if to say, "Of course they are, we paid for a show." The teenage son, however, just looked bored.

The Beach Boys kept coming, their blonde bouffant manes pristine and billowing in the light breeze. They ignored the potential food on the plain, just kept their gazes steady and aimed for the circle of trees that we had come from.

"Ooh this is going to be good," I narrated. "The two groups of brothers have never fought, just stood at the edge of their territories and roared every now and then. But now one of their girls has been stolen. They don't care that she's from a weak pride. She is theirs, and they will not tolerate any other male going near her. A male lion's psyche, in fact most males' psyches, is a fragile thing and depends on the ability to keep females interested. This is going to cause trouble." I was bouncing in my seat, swinging from the direction of the Beach Boys to back over my shoulder, as if I expected the northerners to burst out and face the challenge.

"Who's going to win?" the boy asked. This was a question like who'd win in a fight between a crocodile and an alligator or a killer whale and a shark. There are too many variables to make any answer valid. But I offered my opinion anyway. I thought that the northerners would prevail, because they were huge lions, freakish even. The Beach Boys had numerical supremacy, but they were smaller. One of them was almost a runt. This odd-looking male had noticeably shorter legs than his brothers, and I used to call him the dachshund.

"Okay," the teen said after my answer, and went back to scanning the sky and surrounding bush for an Xbox.

The Beach Boys kept coming, jumping the channels in their path, shaking their manes, and looking more determined than I had ever seen a male lion look. I wanted ringside seats for their meeting with the northerners, so I raced back into the circle of trees and sat on the far side of the trio. The sated male still reposed, his brother still begged, and the female still declined—all unaware of the trouble on the way.

We waited, and I explained to the guests that this would shake up our whole ecosystem. As lions were the apex predator, if males were driven out in the north or south, hyenas would take over that area until new bosses arrived, and the hyenas in turn would drive out cheetahs and wild dogs and force the leopards to hunt only prey that they could drag into trees.

We waited some more. Then the father of the family asked if the other guides had seen anything interesting, and I realized he was as bored as his teenage son. I felt frustrated at his lack of appreciation and started to doubt my own predictions, as the Beach Boys were taking a lot longer to get to the stage than I would have predicted. But then there was a high-pitched call of "Poh!" from the fringe of the island, and baboons shot from their feeding place on the ground into the palms and ebony trees, where they perched and watched the unfolding drama.

"They're coming," I said, breathless in anticipation.

A squat palm bush rustled, and a blonde-fringed face appeared. Another appeared on its left, then one more to its right.

The begging northerner shot a fortuitous glance over his shoulder and spotted them. I expected him to raise his hackles or charge them or roar defiantly, braggingly challenging them like, "I may not have had her, but my brother just did! What do you say to that, blondies?"

Instead he slunk low on his belly to his snoozing brother and nudged him with his nose. The sexual conqueror lazily opened an eye and saw the three stalking out of the bushes onto the white sand.

And ran.

Perhaps his testosterone was depleted by the past few days' activities. He didn't even hesitate, taking off so quickly that his brother was left behind before quickly scurrying after him.

They ran by us, ears flat, tails streaming, shoulders pumping. The Beach Boys came roaring after, right toward us, and the scene of them charging remains to this day the most awe-inspiring sight I have ever seen.

The female who had helped start the clash (and whose pride would be renamed the Matata Pride or Problem Pride forever after) wisely shot off in the opposite direction. I turned the vehicle to pursue the pursuers, launching out of the ring and into a landscape of plains dotted with trees and crisscrossed by gently flowing channels. The lions leapt these, barely visible ahead of us. The northerners had departed with such speed that they were out of view. Two of the Beach Boys were bare specks, but despite the blur of his little legs, the dachshund was only a hundred yards ahead of us.

With the whine of the turbo ringing loud, we overtook him, splashing through water, crashing through bush, and jerking with startling and unusual violence at every gear change. "Mechanical problem!" I shouted into the wind made by our passage, which I would later realize was untrue. In my excitement I had pushed the floor mat up and pinned the accelerator flat, so at each change of the stick shift, we shot forward like a rocket blasting off.

The whiplashed tourists were at last smiling as we snapped ahead. I felt victorious, but then realized that it was not the animals but my wild driving that they were enjoying, as they gave out a whoop after we splashed through every waterway.

The engine glugged after these soakings, and I checked the speedometer. We were doing over forty miles an hour, but were barely gaining on the furious Beach Boys. With no restraint I yelled over the radio to the other guides that if they wanted a spectacle they needed to move at a speed disregarding safety, but they were off looking at other things.

Finally, after a distance of three miles, I admitted defeat. My indomitable Land Rover was no match for the speed and fury of cuckolded lions. And at an impenetrable strand of acacia bush (by now we had moved far from the wetland area and were in a section of Kalahari bushland), I stopped the car and suggested we wash down any dust with a coffee.

I grinned through the first few minutes of our break, not really listening to what anyone was saying, until I hurriedly forced everyone back into the vehicle at the appearance of the dachshund, still running at his top speed. He let out a wheezy roar, letting his brothers know that he was still backing them up, and whirred away into the thorn scrub.

"Go get 'em boy," I said.

■ ▨

Back at camp I regaled any staff member who would listen about the best sighting I had ever had. I was on a high, hopping from one foot to the other as I approached the brunch table.

The father of the family broke away from the group of guests that he had been speaking to. I imagined he must have been telling them about the spectacle he had witnessed and wasn't Africa grand and so on. I beamed at him as he approached.

"Pater," he began. (He had misinterpreted my Australian accent at the start of his stay and called me Pater from the beginning.) "Those others saw a leopard this morning. And a cheetah."

My smile wavered a little. I didn't think guests should be allowed to speak to each other after drives. But it would be hard to build a fence between them, so management always vetoed my suggestion. I thought of telling him that if he visited Europe he wouldn't try to see every museum in a day and what he just witnessed was less than a once in a lifetime experience. But I was sure it was unnecessary. He must understand the value of seeing such a chase.

Then he said, "It looks like you've got some catching up to do."

The World's Worst Bathroom

For a few months I had the world's worst bathroom. My tent was meant to be upgraded, and as a result had been picked up and put down about twenty yards away from where it once stood. This would not have been inconvenient, except that the bathroom section had stayed behind. My new canvas house was to be built abutting it. But the builder did not show up for more than a month. Then when he did arrive, he got malaria within a week and left, and I found myself making midnight dashes to take care of the most private of business.

The reason I was forced to leave my run so late was that one side of the bathroom, the side that I looked out to whilst enthroned, was open to the African air. If my tent had been the last in the line of staff housing, it might have been more acceptable to sit there during daylight hours. But it was the first house, and every other guide and manager had to pass it to get home.

So every night I would wait until I heard conversations cease and watch for lights to go out before scanning the surrounding bush with a flashlight, ascertaining whether the eyes that reflected back belonged to harmless creatures like bush babies and porcupines or more deadly creatures like lions and leopards.

If the coast was clear, I would dash, wearing only shorts and sandals, check for scorpions under the seat (you only need to forget this check once to have it seared into your consciousness—and backside), and do what business needed to be done.

On occasion if I had waited so long, or had been struck by one of the many stomach ailments Africa has, I was a little too perfunctory in my search with the flashlight. Shortly after checking for scorpions one evening, I realized that I had missed something substantially larger. As I sat down, hobbled by my hastily unbuttoned shorts, a buffalo stepped in front of me, close enough to kick if I swung my leg out (which I had no intention of doing). It was as oblivious of me as I clearly had been of it only moments before when I scanned with the light, and it just stood, methodically chewing cud.

I didn't dare make a sound, and I felt the vulnerability that made our forebears first cover themselves with skins and fig leaves. Then, against my will, I made a noise. To my astonishment, the buffalo took off, galloping away into the darkness, frightened by an unfamiliar sound.

Ploop, ploop!

Scars

"But Rich, you've got to have some scars," I said, appalled. "It's almost rude not to." It seemed incomprehensible to me that a guy could live twenty years and have never seen a doctor to get sewn up. These days, in the era of the XBox, I could understand it. But we were of the BMX and skateboard generation and had constantly crashed and fallen off fast-moving objects. At least I had, but then again, I'm markedly uncoordinated. Maybe it was Richard's athleticism that saved him. He was always beating me at mini-basketball, which we played sitting on the kitchen floor during breaks from study. Maybe it was because he didn't want the fuss that is inevitable when you bleed profusely. He was quite shy and soft spoken, but it still didn't seem right to me not to have a few scars.

"You're lucky," he said slyly. "Chicks dig scars." It was the sort of thing he said as a half-joke. He had a longtime crush on a girl named Rebecca, and I and a few of his other friends could not believe how long it was taking him to make a move. We were past the two-year mark, and counting.

The setup we had at the time was very convenient. Richard's parents were overseas for a year, leaving him an apartment that was far superior to what most students had. He was in his last year at university, and I had returned to Australia to finish high school at a day college. We both had the same aim—to get back to Africa and work as safari guides. Richard was born there and had volunteered a few holidays for a safari outfit, while I had a year's experience already but had promised myself that I would finish school one day.

So we studied, ate pizza, and sat on the floor throwing an undersize ball at an undersize hoop. One weekend, the phone rang. It was Richard explaining that he was in the hospital. Excellent—he'll get some scars! I thought. Then I heard the story.

He'd been tripped, by a girl, while playing netball. For those unfamiliar with the sport, it is like a cross between fast-moving basketball and slow-moving tai chi. You can pass the ball, but you are not allowed to run with it. It's a popular sport with girls' schools, because the liability is so limited.

Yet somehow in this softly played game, Richard had broken the larger bone in his thumb, thus successfully one-upping me (at this point I'd had almost a hundred stitches in my life, but no breaks). It was such an awkward spot, the hand required surgery, and Richard was left with a purple and ropey keloid scar on his hand. It was very eye-catching, and for the sake of Richard's pride, I felt it needed a story.

"You cannot, under any circumstances, tell the truth about this," I told him. "You must, I repeat *must*, tell people that you sustained the injury in Africa. Everybody knows that you spend a lot of time there. Tell them that a lion came at you and took a swipe. You fended it off, but one claw hooked you in the thumb. Then, because you are a conservationist, you put it in a sleeper hold until it was unconscious and then walked away."

"I couldn't tell a lie like that," Richard said.

"Well you bloody well should."

Richard was often asked about his scar. And within moments of his mentioning netball, people's eyes would crinkle around the edges, and you could see they were trying not to smile.

A few years later Richard and his fiancé (hooray!) Rebecca ended up working for the same company as me in Botswana. We rarely saw each other, as the camps we worked at were only accessible by air, but we often spoke on the radios, which were our umbilical cords to the world. Every now and then we'd bump into each other at an airstrip as we came or went from our leave, or we might spend a night or two at the other's camp.

It's a strange way to maintain a friendship, and I was sometimes in as frequent contact with my sister in Sydney as I was with Richard and Rebecca.

When the radio call of an incident came through, my leave was just starting and I was visiting a camp called Xigera. Robyn, a Canadian girl who was working there, came to tell me that Richard had been attacked by a lion.

"Nah," I dismissed it, "It was just netball. Glad to hear he's using the story though."

It took some convincing, but eventually I went to the structure that served as an office, and the usually crackling and ceaseless chatter of the radio was absent. This was unheard of. With almost twenty camps around Northern Botswana all using the same frequency, there was always some manager on the radio insisting that eggs get put on the next flight or requesting a seat on a plane out to see the dentist or asking for a guide because theirs was sick. But now there was only the hiss of empty airwaves. Every now and then it would burst into life as someone spoke of mede-vac planes or where the bloody hell was the nurse, and I knew Robyn had been telling the truth. I was desperate to speak to someone to find out what was going on, but knew that all I would do was hinder the arrangements that were being made. It was only much later that anyone could find out what had happened.

■ ■

The night before, the lions had been roaring in Savuti Camp. Guides always feel that the lions are conspiring against us when they do this, because as the sun comes up they always manage to disappear into bush too thick to follow, leaving your many guests disappointed and convinced that you have absolutely no idea what you are doing. After the guests have been woken up (if they haven't spent the night alert and in unnecessary terror), they will say as they sip their coffee, "That was lions, right? Outside my tent! Right outside my tent!"

One of the other guests will pipe up and say, "No, actually the lions were right outside *my* tent." If you are feeling finicky, you can explain that a lion's roar travels up to four miles, and that the lions they heard were actually a few hundred yards away at the closest. Generally, though, you let them have their fun as you try to coerce them into the vehicles, knowing that every wasted moment puts the lions farther away from you.

Richard had only one couple in his vehicle on the day he was attacked. They were excited about the lions, even though they had been on safari many times before. They set off in the Land Rover, following the tracks of a lioness that had conveniently (and not unusually) chosen to walk along one of the dirt roads. When you first set out, you know that no matter how skillful a tracker you are, no matter your ability to read the signs of the bush like alarm calls, it is still a lottery. If the lion decides it is hot, it may flop right beside a termite mound in full view, making it easy to find, or it may slink into deep, gnarled woodland where no vehicle can follow and it is unsafe to go in on foot.

This lioness seemed to have enjoyed a long walk along the road, and Richard followed her tracks for close to a mile before they abruptly turned into the long grass, heading straight for an impenetrable stand of trees. He stepped out of the vehicle to take a better look at the tracks.

They were fresh, not steaming as we often said, but fresh enough that if she had come back to the road somewhere farther down, he might still find her.

He was tracking in a riverbed that has been dry for more than twenty years, leaving a snaking swathe of grassland through woodland that is otherwise featureless for hundreds of miles. Termite mounds and the occasional shrub dot the river of grass. Richard scanned these and took a few more steps in the lioness's prints, which carried on straight to the thick forest ahead of him. He squatted down, looking closer at the tracks and realizing he probably wasn't going to find the lion. Because his head was down, it was only when he heard his guests scream that he knew something was wrong. She was coming.

The lioness must have doubled back and had been resting on the other side of the termite mound closest to Richard. Later we would discover that she was alone because she had recently given birth to little cubs, and lionesses always split from the pride for a few weeks when this happens. She was a first-time mother, probably a little unsure of all her responsibilities, and Richard had unfortunately chosen to get out at the very place she had her cubs hidden. There are few things as dangerous in the world as a lioness that thinks her cubs are threatened.

As soon as he heard the warning, Richard stood up and made himself as large as he possibly could, raising his arms and shouting. This is exactly the right thing to do, and it works nearly every time.

This lioness didn't follow the rules. A lion may stop within terrifying inches from you at the end of a mock charge, right at the point you are convinced you have had it. So the standard advice is to stay facing the animal so that it thinks you are going to fight. Somehow, at the last split-second, Richard saw that she wasn't doing a mock charge and spun, so she hit him from behind. The lioness was young, so probably weighed about two hundred and fifty pounds, the size of a very large man, but she was running at twice the speed of an Olympic sprinter when she slammed into him, and the impact was strong enough to dislocate his right shoulder.

He landed facedown, lying over his good arm, his wounded shoulder and arm out to the side. The lion bit into the shoulder, trying to figure out where she should go to choke him. Lions eat mainly quadrupeds, so a human's structure confuses them. She then bit into the back of his head, taking out a piece the size of a Porterhouse steak at the very top of his neck. She raked his back, and one claw somehow sliced from his chin up into his mouth, cutting into his palate, while another took off his ear, leaving it hanging by a flap of a skin.

Through all this, he knew he should fight, but his good arm was underneath him, and with the lion on his back he couldn't free it. His dislocated arm was useless to hit the lion with, but he tried anyway. Later the couple in the vehicle would say that his arm's flicking back and forth as he tried to punch distracted the lion every time she was about to bite him again.

The woman in the vehicle screamed at her husband to get behind the wheel and drive at the lion, which probably saved Richard's life. When the Land Rover approached, the lion got off Richard and backed away, crouching low as if to say, "Come out and try to get him."

But Richard managed to stand up of his own accord and staggered into the passenger side of the vehicle. He radioed for help, and another guide from the camp came and picked up Richard and his terrified guests.

Once he was back in camp, bleeding and in deep shock, Rebecca did what a nurse would later describe as a miraculous job of applying first aid. A helicopter would have been the most direct way to get him out, but there were no sober helicopter pilots available that morning, so Richard had to take an extremely bumpy ride over the rutted track to the airstrip. From there a plane took him to Gaborone, Botswana's capital city.

Richard's parents immediately flew out from London to be with their son and to transfuse blood they knew was uninfected after Rebecca had given all she safely could. There was no doubt that Richard was in for a long recovery.

The hospitals in Botswana are better than many people might imagine. Richard would, however, need to go to Johannesburg for a good plastic surgeon. Because of the high road toll and stupendous number of firearms in that city, reconstructive surgeons are in high demand and have a wealth of experience. And these surgeons all want an animal attack in their portfolios (yes, they have portfolios, with before and after photos). In their industry, it's glamorous. Buffalo and hippo damage are okay, but a lion attack is the trump card. Richard was faced with a buffet of medicos.

Eventually Richard settled on a surgeon, who did immaculate work. By the time Richard and Rebecca were married a few years later, he was well healed. His ear had been reattached, and his hair had grown over the skin graft on the back of his head. A thin white line traveled up his chin but was barely noticeable. Only if his shirt was off would you register that something big and bad had done him harm.

In fact when people have known Richard long enough now to feel they can ask him, they say, "Man, how'd you get that scar on your hand?"

His answer is still the same. "Netball."

Khama: A Love Story

Perhaps one of the oldest traditions on safari, maybe even in Africa, is to sit around the fire at night and tell stories. It usually starts with a tourist asking a question like, "What's the most dangerous animal you've encountered?"

The stories that follow are enjoyable to tell and hear, and leave people breathless. But my favorite story to tell around a campfire is about the man who made Botswana the country it is. The surprise is that the story is not a history lesson or about politics. It is a love story.

■ ■

Sir Seretse Khama was born in the town of Serowe, which looks more like a village than a town to anyone from the Western world. He was not a sir when he was born, of course, that only came later. And it is surprising that it happened at all, considering that for many years the British did everything they could to stop him from becoming a man of any importance.

He was only four years old when his father died, an important event in the life of any man, but even more so for the young Seretse, as his father was kgosi, or king, of the Batawana people.

This is the name of the main tribe in what is now Botswana. In those days it was a British protectorate and called Bechuanaland. It was sensibly decided that Seretse was too young to rule. His uncle, Tshekedi, took over as regent until he was old enough to be kgosi, and young Seretse was sent to South Africa to be educated. After school he was sent to England, where he started to study at Oxford. In 1947 he met a young Englishwoman named Ruth Williams at a dance arranged by the London Missionary Society (LMS). By accounts, there was nothing extraordinary about their meeting, nor anything to foretell what would become of them. All they seemed to have in common was a liking for jazz.

Somewhere in his disparate life, though, Seretse had acquired a great wit, unshakeable integrity, and an obvious intelligence. Perhaps it was these things that impressed Ruth, for within the year Seretse proposed, and she accepted.

This created a storm that neither the young but wise Seretse nor the London girl Ruth could have foreseen. When Seretse sent news to his uncle that he was not only marrying outside the tribe, but marrying a white English woman Tshekedi was apoplectic.

Tshekedi in pictures looks quite normal, even pleasant, but at this stage he showed himself to be quite a ruthless schemer, of the variety usually found in fables like the "The Arabian Nights." He demanded Seretse take back the proposal. Seretse refused and instead moved forward the date of the wedding in case his uncle somehow plotted against it—a wise move, as Tshekedi had already wired the society that had arranged the fateful dance and demanded they intervene. Appalled at the prospect of having created any sort of scandal, the LMS brought the pressure it could to bear on whomever it could influence, which was a group of people and institutions of great importance. But it was not just uncle Tshekedi and the LMS who didn't want the marriage to go ahead. The British government had also decided the union would present a problem for them. World War II had cost them dearly in so many ways, one of which was financially. They were in desperate need of uranium and gold, and their main supplies came from South Africa. It was the start of the Apartheid era, and the British were told that if they allowed a black king to marry a white woman, they were asking for trouble in the form of trade sanctions (a threat that could be considered ironic considering how many nations were becoming uneasy about trading with them). A report was commissioned in England to show that Seretse was unfit to lead his people. But to the ire of the government, the presiding judge found the exact opposite and stated that he was as well suited as anyone to be kgosi.

The report was stuffed away in a drawer somewhere, and it stayed there for thirty years.

Meanwhile, the star-crossed lovers were yet to have their wedding. When Seretse and Ruth went to be married, the vicar bowed to pressure from the LMS and refused them a service. Indomitable, resolute, and in love, they went to the bishop of London.

He refused to marry them too.

Public interest in their case rose, and criticisms of the government began. At the same time that the English government was hearing these condemnations, a secret agent was dispatched to whisper in Seretse's ear that Ruth was actually a communist agent sent to distract him. He sensibly ignored this madness and continued trying to find a way to marry the woman he loved.

Fortunately there was no reason for the registry office to refuse, as no laws existed forbidding the marriage of an African prince and an English woman. They were finally wed in 1948, and Seretse returned to Botswana with his wife. There was no joyous homecoming. Instead, his uncle immediately called him to a kgotla. The kgotla is a traditional meeting of the community, normally held in a circular reed-enclosed structure. It is a particularly democratic way for everyone to have his or her say, as nobody can be refused the opportunity to speak on an issue (and everybody, it seems, wants to speak—even if it is to say exactly what his or her neighbor said). Tshekedi claimed that Seretse had moved against his people by marrying a white woman. With a prepared emphatic speech, Tshekedi had Seretse stripped of all royal title.

The kgotla had gone on for four days (they really do speak a lot at these things), but Seretse somehow convinced everyone that another should be held. At the second kgotla Seretse was persuasive, stating that he "could not, and would not, give up his wife" but was nevertheless still loyal to his people. The community stayed on side with Tshekedi. Seretse called for a third kgotla, and something about Tshekedi's desperation to get rid of Seretse made everyone realize that he only wanted the title of kgosi for himself.

Tshekedi challenged the community, proclaiming that they must listen to him as he had been their ruler for so long. If they returned Seretse's title, he told them, he would leave them forever. After thirty years he clearly expected to be revered, but Seretse was enormously popular and was reinstated as paramount chief of the Batawana tribe. Tshekedi left the country, and with him out of the picture Seretse returned to his studies.

Soon Ruth was pregnant, and Seretse was elated. They had

overcome the British government, defeated the aims of his uncle, completed his studies, and could now settle in Botswana. Shortly after moving back, Seretse was asked back to Britain as a representative of his people, and he graciously accepted even though he suspected some ulterior motives. Once in England he was told by government officials that he would not be allowed to return to Botswana. He was to consider himself in exile. Ruth was still in Botswana, a new land for her, pregnant and alone. Using all of his diplomacy and the support of those in England who were appalled at the way he and his wife were being treated (this group included people such as Winston Churchill, who had done a backflip after originally describing their union as "problematic"), he was able to come home for the birth of their child, a daughter named Jacqueline Tebogo Khama. Then the government bundled the whole family back to England and told them they were there to stay.

There was now greater outcry over their treatment and the pandering to a clearly racist regime. Yet in 1952 it was announced that their exile was not to be temporary and must remain permanent. Seretse, Ruth, and their family would never be allowed back to Africa.

After four years of international condemnation, the English government capitulated, allowing the Khamas back to Botswana. But there was one condition: They were to return as commoners, giving up any claim to leading the Batawana. After a very challenging nine-year relationship, one might expect that Ruth would want to stay in the country of her birth, but she stood by Seretse and accompanied him to Botswana.

This was an age where many African colonies were pushing for independence from their European masters, and some were openly revolting. Seretse had been a thorn in the side of the British for years, and the South African government despised him. They perhaps expected Seretse to agitate and therefore be easy to imprison, getting him out of the way for good. But as if to foil them once more, he quietly took up cattle ranching.

It was a job that he seemed peculiarly bad at.

After several years of losing money, and cattle (which to an African man is the same thing, even if he went to Oxford), he gave up his cowboy ways and started the Bechuanaland Democratic Party in 1962. By now he and Ruth had had a brother for Jacqueline, named Ian, then twin boys, one of whom was named Anthony. The other reflected Seretse's policy of forgiveness and was named Tshekedi.

Seretse pushed for peaceful change from Botswana's "protected" status and proposed racial unity and tolerance as a way to build the country. He gained the respect of regional leaders, and in 1965 he was made prime minister of Botswana by the English, but was in the strange position of being unable to travel to its capital. This was because the whole country was in the even stranger position of not having a capital within its borders. Instead the British administered it from a town called Mafeking, in South Africa. Seretse had been warned that if he ever went there, he would be arrested immediately by the South African government for marrying a white woman.

A new capital, Gaborone, was hastily declared and built. It was located a stone's throw from Mafeking but this time within Botswana's borders. In many African countries the English were finding themselves the targets of violence, as resentment against colonialism built. They started looking at Seretse in a different light. He was a man who had always promoted racial unity and working together for the cause of the country. So in a reversal of attitudes, Seretse was welcomed in Gaborone by the English administrators and was even knighted by Queen Elizabeth II in 1966. Ruth, once a clerk, became Lady Mohumagadi Mma Kgosi Ruth Khama. This was a regal title befitting the queen that she briefly had been, but she was always affectionately known by the population as Lady K.

European countries were shedding their colonies (unless they made them lots of money), and as Botswana only had protectorate status and was one of the world's poorest nations, it was one of the first in line to be granted freedom. The British had only agreed to take it over in the first place so that the Germans couldn't have it, and they were now quite willing to let it go.

A story from this time, often repeated by the people of Botswana but rarely seen in history books, illustrates that even after all his trials, Seretse maintained a sense of humor. This was remarkable, as he was often insulted during the transitional period. Every time something went wrong with the process, the outgoing authorities would complain of a "nigger in the woodpile." Seretse bore it, and when he was elected as the nation's first president on September 30, 1966, reporters asked him many inane questions. One of the inquiries was whether he intended to change the name of the manor that once housed the colonial administrators but would now be the presidential residence. "Yes," he replied. "I'll be calling it the Woodpile."

Seretse immediately set about arranging Botswana's economic future. He struck a deal with the European Community for Botswana's beef industry and promised that the profits belonged to the people of Botswana. To ensure these profits actually went to the people, and not into politicians' pockets, he established trusts, the interest from which went into health, education, and infrastructure. In a move that marked him as very different from many other African leaders, he also established a vigorous anticorruption unit. And to this day Botswana is one of the few countries in Africa where bribes don't settle the majority of "problems."

Ruth was just as busy. She started the first branches of many charities in Botswana, including the Red Cross. While it is often stated that she stayed away from Seretse's political activities, there is no doubt that they shared an ideology, which centered around helping and advancing the people of the country they both loved.

Just months after independence, Seretse received incredible news. In a place called Orapa, diamond deposits had been discovered—big diamond deposits. Within months Botswana was one of the world's leading producers of the gemstone. Refreshingly for the region these were mined without any military involvement, making them "clean" and desirable to buyers of conscience. With the economic structures set in place by Seretse, the country flourished.

In fact from 1966 until 1980, Botswana had the world's fastest growing economy. The diamonds made the difference. But for once in an African country, money was spent on providing free health care and education. Medical insurance is close to free, and income tax is zero.

In the years that the country he led was flourishing, Seretse was often seriously ill. He had a pacemaker fitted in the 1970s, but his medical troubles were not over. In 1980, as he worked toward independence for Rhodesia and a Southern African Development

Community, he died from cancer. The country mourned in a way rarely seen for a president, or for a king, or the rare man that had been both.

Many people expected Lady K to return to England, but she was now a Motswana (the term for a citizen of Botswana), as were her children. She stayed in Botswana, the country she and Seretse had loved as much as each other. In 2002 she died, and joined Seretse, perhaps in a place where they play jazz.

Beau Goes Back to Nature

The monkeys at Mombo were a problem, but the baboons were not. We waged a deliberate campaign against them nevertheless—not harming them but making sure that they never became so comfortable in the camp as to become pests.

However, the camp was within their home range, and the whole troop would frequently cross the plain that fronted the camp and forage beneath and in the trees that shaded the tents. Among the troop was one of the strangest animals I have ever seen, even odder than Martina the hairy lioness or the stripeless zebra at Duba.

At the time, there was a nudist in South Africa who had gained an unreasonable amount of prominence. He went by the unlikely name of Beau Brummel. Since the strange baboon amongst the Mombo troop did not have a single hair, not even an eyelash, I named him Beau.

Beau the nudist baboon had skin the color of dark chocolate, shiny and tight. His lack of fur made his orange yellow eyes beacons. Often as the troop foraged near the camp, I would notice him sitting on his backside, arms resting on his knees, as he watched the humans moving around. Maybe he saw something familiar in our hairless forms and wondered why he couldn't join us. Maybe he was just doing what all baboons do, and I only noticed him because he was naked. Either way, he never made an attempt to become human (although in a strange moment of voyeurism he was caught peeking at a female staff member as she showered), and the troop didn't seem to ostracize him. He fed with them, moved when they did, and on a number of occasions I saw him copulating—something baboons do openly, noisily, and often.

Beau's condition did mean that he missed out on one of the most important parts of a baboon's social activity. He would groom others, meticulously parting their fur and removing any ticks or fleas that he found, biting them before carrying on his salon treatment. But the favor could not be returned. Maybe this endeared him to certain lazy members of the troop, but it would have made him feel left out. Females groom to show affection; males do it to show allegiance. If another baboon wanted to groom Beau, all he could do was glance over him once, pat him on his bald rump, and say "All clear, buddy!"

One morning I found another way that his nudity impaired him. As usual I was the first guide to make it to the deck and was swallowing a cup of coffee that the even earlier rising kitchen staff had prepared. I scanned the plain, in the vain hope that some predator might make my life easy by being perched on a termite mound, and settled my eye on the baboons that were moving, softly grunting, and feeding around the deck. A distance apart sat Beau, clutching his knees and shivering. He was cold. I'd never seen an animal's teeth chatter before, and my heart went out to him. I would have given him a blanket if I could, but he would have run away at any approach, and all he would do with a blanket was tear it up anyway. Baboons are smart, but not geniuses. Eventually he went and sat next to a female baboon, huddling against her. But she had a baby to feed, so she got up and walked away. He tried to get warmth from a young male who also moved on, then Beau sat back down, shaking and looking miserable, the gleam in his eyes dimmed.

Beau's lack of insulation probably made him more susceptible to colds and flu, and despite the darkness of his skin, he would have suffered frequent sunburns. But I watched him on and off for years; he showed no signs of ill health and it looked like he would lead a full life.

About a year after I left Mombo to manage a camp farther north, I was speaking to a guide named Greg, who had taken over for me.

"I saw Beau the other day," he told me. "By himself." Baboons are never alone, so something must have happened for him to be driven out or left behind. I was worried for him.

Greg explained that Beau had come down to a channel to drink, nervously looking for a spot where a crocodile couldn't grab him.

He should have been looking behind him.

A leopard we knew as the Bird Island Female barreled out of a palm clump and, with the remarkable efficiency of her species, killed him almost as soon as he knew something was wrong.

Damn, I thought. If it had been any other baboon, I would have asked Greg about how close they were, how good the viewing had been, and how his guests reacted. A lot of people come to Africa hoping to see some action, namely a predator making a kill. Guides are normally happy to show this, but when the victim is an animal that you have known, and named, it is like losing a friend. We reflected on this, not mentioning the hundreds of animals that we had seen get devoured and never cared for. Then Greg told me that the sighting hadn't ended with the kill. The leopard had barely begun to feed when a hyena appeared. Hissing and snarling, the leopard gave up her prize. The hyena had only enough time to drag Beau's body to a bush and start cracking his bones for the rich marrow within when lions appeared. They drove the hyena off, quickly devouring what was left and moving on, the portion so small they didn't even stop to rest after their meal.

"That would have been a great sighting, and I'd be envious," I said, "if it wasn't Beau."

"Yeah," Greg said. "I didn't like it at all."

What we both knew was that this was Africa, where life is often short and brutal. We didn't really try to console each other. We both blustered about how dangerous it is to get attached to a wild animal, for if anything, Beau's demise and extraordinary distribution just served to illustrate that in the end, we all go back to nature.

Mona Lisa

Each year, Pierre would bring a group on safari. Despite his French name, he was South African born and bred, but like so many people had relocated from his beloved homeland during the Apartheid era. He was successful in America, and as a way of paying something back to the continent of his birth, he brought out groups of friends on safari every year and gave the profits of the trip to an African charity.

I looked forward to his groups, as the people he brought were usually deeply interested in conservation and a pleasure to take on safari. This year he brought a group into a camp that perched on the banks of the Linyanti River. I was temporarily managing the camp and having a brief hiatus from full-time guiding. The river that flows by it forms the border of Namibia and Botswana and is a graceful series of swooping turns and oxbow lagoons, filled with snorting hippos and basking crocodiles.

As Pierre's group pulled into the camp, I spotted potential trouble. One of the women was "dressed" for safari. Her handbag had the name of someone Italian in large letters on it, and the jacket she wore was made from the skin of some supple and probably endangered animal. There was not a crease in any of her clothing—an impressive feat, considering they had just arrived in a cramped light aircraft. Everything she wore was an unfashionable khaki or brown, but the entire ensemble was clearly worth more than the Land Rover she was riding in. The sunglasses alone could have shaded an African village.

As we entered the main area of the camp, she sniffed, and to her credit managed to squeeze through gritted teeth the words, "How lovely."

I kept an eye on her during the stay to make sure she was enjoying herself, and she seemed to appreciate the recommendation I gave her not to put anything delicate in our laundry, as it was manned by tough women who treated stains as a mortal enemy and would rub a garment to threads if unchecked.

This seemed to endear me to her, and she often sat next to me at mealtimes. To my surprise I found that I enjoyed her company. She just wasn't an animal person, she said. She didn't dislike them, but they held no real interest for her. This was strange to me, because I couldn't imagine not getting a thrill out of seeing an elephant in the wild, even if I had seen them thousands of times before.

She hadn't really been interested in the trip, she explained, but her husband was a friend of Pierre's and liked animals, so she had come along. In exchange for her smiling endurance of Africa, she and her husband were going to tour Europe and its galleries and museums the next year.

"You know that the money from this trip is going to some fund to save rhinos, don't you?" she asked me.

I affirmed that I did, and she asked another question: "What does it matter if the rhinos die out? Is it really important that they are saved?" This would normally have riled me, and I would have normally given a snappish answer, but I had come to think of her as Dr. Spock from *Star Trek*—an emotionless, purely logical creature, at least with regards to her feelings for animals. Like Spock, though, I knew there were one or two things that stirred her, so I gave an honest reply. "If the rhinos are gone, maybe there is a dung beetle that feeds only on their droppings. It dies out, so does a bird that feeds on it, and that bird stops spiders from getting out of hand but now has an imbalanced diet and dies out." She didn't looked concerned by this, but I still had my trump card. "But to be honest, it doesn't matter. No economy will suffer, nobody will go hungry, no diseases will be spawned. Yet there will never be a way to place a value on what we have lost. Future children will see rhinos only in books and wonder how we let them go so easily. It would be like lighting a fire in the Louvre and watching the Mona Lisa burn. Most people would think 'What a pity' and leave it at that while only a few wept."

She smiled at the end of my soliloquy and said, "When we leave I could give you a tip, or add it to our donation to the rhino thingy. Which would you prefer?" She had me over a barrel. My wages were insignificant, and I lived for my tips. But I had always claimed that I wasn't in the job for the money, and in all honesty only a fool would be.

So I returned the smile and said, "Save Mona."

Bird Nerds

At nineteen years old, as I made preparations to head to Africa for the first time, I sat with my friend Richard, who already had safari experience. He was giving me a run through on things I should know. He pointed out that cheetahs have a long, lithe body built for speed, whereas leopards are stockier and more powerful. He explained that the white rhinoceros has a square mouth for cropping grass, while the black rhino has a hook lip for gripping leaves.

Then Richard opened a massive book, the sort that would break bones if it were dropped on your foot, and showed me pictures that appalled me. The page was filled with seemingly identical birds with brown feathers. There was nothing about them that was in the least bit interesting, and I couldn't imagine what sort of person would want to pay attention to them. I listened halfheartedly as Richard explained that while they might look exactly the same, the trained ear could determine their species by call and the expert observer could also use flight pattern as a clue. At one point he paused and asked if there was something wrong with my eyes, as they had glazed over.

"Early onset cataracts," I lied, not wanting to offend. "Tragically common in my family."

I was going to Africa for the animals. My perception was

that people who watched birds wore funny clothes and had poor hygiene. They had beards (even the women) with bits of food stuck in them. Bird-watching was close kin to the dirty perversions of stamp collecting and crocheting cushion covers. I loved all nature, and regularly fed wild parrots in my backyard, but if someone had suggested I was a bird-watcher, I would have cringed and insisted that I was no such thing. Only people who couldn't engage in normal activities like bike riding and seeing movies looked at birds and spent time ticking off the ones they had seen. I was a young teen when I started feeding the parrots and was becoming increasingly convinced that one day I might like to meet a girl and have sex. Being a bird-watcher, I was sure, would guarantee that it would never happen.

Fortunately, once I had moved to South Africa and had my first job in the safari industry, I realized that most tourists came to see animals that could kill them but hopefully wouldn't. When people listed what they wanted to see—as if ordering from a menu—it would typically go something like this: "Lions. Have to see lions, preferably hunting something. Any other cats would be good too, and some elephants and hippos. Maybe a zebra or giraffe for dessert would be nice."

Rarely would birds feature on the list and then only hesitatingly as an addendum. "Yes, and if, you know, we, um, well, see some birds, I wouldn't mind, you know, having a quick look. That's only if everybody else is okay with that?"

Some guides were proud of their bird knowledge and could give as much detailed information about the fork-tailed drongo as they could the elephant. They gave the impression they were better guides than me for having this knowledge. And so I would point out the handful of birds that I could identify of the more than nine hundred species that occur in Southern Africa, sticking to the brightly colored ones that didn't need a lifetime's worth of study or a fear of sexual rejection to identify. Occasionally, to show the depth of my knowledge, I would shout, "Ostrich!" and say a few words about this most conspicuous bird, thus proving to myself that I was a well-rounded guide and not just a mammal guy.

After two years in South Africa, I moved to the Okavango Delta in Botswana. It is one of the planet's most spectacular and beautiful places, wild and open beyond anything I'd ever seen. It felt like a playground for wildlife. But even amidst the eye-popping abundance of antelopes and predators, the birds stood out. There were so many, in such variety, with such color, that they could not be brushed aside.

I started looking at my book.

Then I put some ticks next to the species I'd seen.

I am not becoming one of those people, I insisted to myself.

Soon after, I spent one whole afternoon with some drab wading birds, figuring out whether they were wood sandpipers or common sandpipers. They were brown and boring looking, but the challenge of figuring out what they were suddenly excited me. I took a nerdish thrill in using the clues, such as how far a patch of white extended up the shoulder or whether the back was speckled or spotted (a fine distinction) to determine the bird's true identity. When I figured out what they were, I felt a triumph that never came from something as obvious as knowing the difference between a zebra and a giraffe.

I was hooked, and it didn't take long before I went on vacation to a place just because of the birds that could be found there.

Within a year I overheard somebody say in answer to a query, "Ask Peter, he knows birds."

"No I don't!" I felt like saying, wanting to preserve whatever sexual appeal I might have, but instead I started to point out the bird's identifying features to the hapless tourist, who had only been asking for the sake of something to say. I stopped when I saw he or she had suddenly developed an eye problem.

It reached a point that the safaris I led contained as much information about birds as animals. But I found that by sticking to extreme behavior or unusual evolutionary tactics, people seemed interested. Or perhaps they were just being polite. Either way I was pretty sure that I had become a bird nerd, one of those people.

I started looking forward to, and chose to, guide the groups who had marked a specific interest in birds. They were rare, because our camp's selling point was generally larger animals, which we had in unusual abundance, and people can see birds anywhere. But every now and then, we would have a booking that had a note, "interested in birds." Sometimes a bunch of birders would flock together so they could get a group discount and land at our camp. These would usually arrive in summer, when the number of bird species was at its highest and most regular, and animals-only tourists were driven away by the likelihood of rain.

One group traveled with a well-known ornithologist (okay, well-known if you are a bird nerd) who gave a little pep talk to his group before we set out on our first drive: "There are two types of people who start watching birds. Those who have a love of nature that extends to all living things, and those who like lists and feel the need to get a whole set. Enjoy the birds, but take the time to enjoy the elephants and the insects and everything in between as well."

These people may have been bird nerds, but they behaved in a way and were normal looking enough to suggest that at some point they may have even had sex. Over three days we saw just more than two hundred species of birds, including many firsts for my list, like Ayre's eagle and pink-throated longclaw, and fantastic wildlife as well. Ironically, birders usually see the best game. Because they are looking for anything small and moving, they often spot things like the tip of a leopard's tail as it flicks or the slow flap of an elephant's ear deep in the thick bush. The group made an excited and appreciative babble at every living thing we saw, whether it was big, small, rare, common, feathered, or furred. I am one of these people, I thought, and it didn't seem such a bad thing after all.

Not all groups, though, were as easy to please, or pleasing to be with. Before people arrived at our camp, we knew little about them except their names and which travel agency they had booked through. Occasionally there would be a footnote, such as "allergic to all shellfish, nuts, fruit, lactose, and oxygen," that would drive the woman in charge of catering into a psychopathic rage.

On one booking sheet that summer was a group of four, from England, who were coming specifically for birds. I was almost due leave, and after three months of guiding people who were often bitter that there was not a lion killing something around every corner, I eagerly anticipated three days of a more soft, downy pace. Sitting at the airstrip, waiting for the plane, I imitated some calls to see what birds would answer. I got responses from a pearl-spotted owl, a groundscraper thrush, and Julius, another guide, who was under a different tree mocking me for doing what he considered "work" while I didn't have any guests with me.

Eventually the little plane touched down, spitting mud from its tires. The people peering out the spattered windows were all cut from the same mold and appeared to have gone out of their way to fulfill the stereotype of the nerdish bird-watcher. Floppy hats and steamed-up glasses perched lopsidedly on pale faces. They all wore raincoats in varying shades of brown, and one of the guys had visible finger marks where he had wiped something on his lapel. I doubted that any of them had ever had sex in their lives.

"'Ello, I'm Jill," said the first out of the plane. "And that's Jamie," she said, pointing to a man who was raising his binoculars as he stepped out of the Cessna. This is a bad idea, because you have to step down when exiting a light aircraft, and soon he was sprawled in a puddle. Fortunately he was unconcerned about his dignity and only worried that his precious binoculars might be damaged. Having ascertained that they were not, he introduced me to the other two, who had stoutly British names that I can't remember but were something like Basil and Rosemary.

"We're awfully excited," said Jill. "It's our first time." Then she scrabbled at something around her neck, and I thought she was choking. "Oh my god!" she spluttered, as she finally disentangled herself from her binocular straps. "It's a francolin! Jamie, it's our very first francolin!" A francolin is a species of plump little bird, like an oversize quail. This one cocked an eye at them, scratched at the dirt, then shat. The group cooed happily.

I looked them over and thought, "These are my people. I am one of them."

I explained that I was also an avid bird-watcher and was looking forward to the next few days. I heard a sound like "humph" from the back of the vehicle, ignored it, and started the engine.

The drive back to camp was excruciating. Normally it took less than ten minutes, but with people on their first trip to Africa you had to expect to stop for them to see their first impala, and you could be guaranteed of their excitement if a giraffe made its stately way past you. Sometimes the tourists would get extremely lucky and see an elephant or lion by the tracks on the way back.

This group made me stop for every bird.

Every . . . single . . . one.

In the Okavango you can't drive past a tree (which are plentiful), bush (abundant), or patch of earth (omnipresent) that does not have some sort of birdlife in it, under it, or on it. I wouldn't have minded these pauses at all, except the group were the bird-watching equivalent of extremists. They did not, under any circumstances, want me to help them identify the birds they were seeing. What made this so painful is that they appeared to have memories like goldfish and would spend ten minutes painstakingly recording a bird's identifying features, confirm its type, then stop at the next bush and repeat the process with an individual of the same species. Jamie and Jill did this with vocal excitement, "Oh my! A titbabbler! How marvelous!" On the other hand, Basil and Rosemary took it all in grimly, sternly marking their lists with each identification. I wondered if some predetermined number of sightings was for them a grand British landmark, like defeating Germany.

Once we finally made it back to the camp, all four of my charges had circular indents around their eyes from the binoculars. I left them to settle in, had my Land Rover washed, and waited until four o'clock in the afternoon, when we would head back out on our first official game drive.

Guides give a standard safety talk before heading out on the first drive. Jamie and Jill listened with a grinning intensity throughout the talk. Basil and Rosemary, sitting in the back, frowned in concentration—until we reached the part about potentially dangerous animals, when they both smiled for the first time. Somehow it looked patronizing—as if they had a secret.

At the conclusion of my talk, I started the engine and put the vehicle into first. "Stop! Stop!" roared Basil, who I was beginning to suspect was a little deaf. "Bird!" he added unnecessarily, as the sound of his bellowing voice was driving a swarm of birds and other living things away from us, at speed. I'm convinced that even the earthworms dug deeper. We sat in the turning circle of the camp for the first hour of our drive, the engine off, recording the avifauna around us. Eventually I suggested that we move a little farther out and informed them that the other guides had seen and radioed in something interesting not far from where we were. I also explained that we would need to drive for about ten minutes without too many pauses, but assured them that if I saw any birds they were unlikely to view again, I would stop.

"What have they seen?" asked Jill.

"Some lions feeding on a buffalo," I answered, resignedly giving away what I thought would have been a nice surprise.

There was a cough from the back. I was starting to suspect that Rosemary was mute, so knew it must be Basil. "Would you like to see some lions, everyone?" I asked.

Jamie and Jill both said, "Oh yes, please," their faces flushing.

"We're here for the birds!" bellowed Basil.

"That's settled then," I said. I fired up the cold engine and pulled away a touch faster than I needed to. Muttering from the backseat complemented the diesel engine as we passed any number of birds I didn't pause for, knowing that the group had already recorded them. As we neared where the lions were gorging, I turned to Basil, whose mouth had retreated in pursed disapproval beneath his moustache, and said, "There will be vultures." There was a flicker of a smile, but he caught it in time and stuffed it back under his facial hair.

We sat with the lions until dark, watching them, the vultures, and the birds eating the flies around the vultures. Once I was convinced they couldn't see anymore, I raced back into camp, late for our curfew.

"That was jolly nice, thank you," said Jill and Jamie.

"Humph," said Basil, which could have meant anything. Rosemary just smiled meekly.

The next two days passed in almost the same manner. We never got very far from the camp, which I regretted, because Mombo has so many beautiful places, such as pools filled with hippos and wide-open plains that stretch for miles. But we did see a lot of birds. Every now and then an animal would rudely intrude and amble through as we were determining if what we were looking at was a fan-tailed or black-backed cisticola. Basil would "humph" at the creature, but Jamie and Jill took guilty pleasure from their illicit viewing. I was convinced that they were closeted lovers of nature as a whole and wished that I could have shown them a few more animals. But I was resigned to Basil's bullying.

At mealtimes people might sit next to my group once. But after Basil loudly announced, "All your beasts are fine and well, but we are here for birds!" few people sat near him again. I started putting them at the end of the table whenever I could. And I tried to create a buffer between them and everyone else by posting myself and another guide on the seats next to them. I felt the need to protect whatever image bird-watchers might have. After all, I thought ashamedly, I *am* one of these people.

On our very last drive together, we were making our tortuous pace along a typical Okavango scene, with a wide-open plain dotted with palm clumps on one side and a ribbon of thick riverine forest on the other. It is a haven for life of all types, and I saw something that made me slam on the brakes, which at the speed we were going had very little effect.

"Why?" asked Jamie, a deeper question than I could answer.

"Humph," said Basil.

I took it as an invitation to speak expansively. "So far you have seen a lot of Burchell's starling, right? And a few long-tailed starlings?" They nodded. "And we got lucky and saw a male plum-colored starling in breeding plumage and a greater blue-eared, but as far as I remember you haven't seen a single wattled starling, is that right?" There was a quick consultation of lists, but while I can't remember what I have eaten for breakfast most mornings, I never forget what I have seen with people, so knew I was correct.

"Indeed," said Jamie. And when Basil added his expected "humph," I carried on. "Straight ahead, in that thick patch of forest, is a tree with yellow bark. It's called a sycamore fig, which probably won't interest you. But if you follow up its main trunk, you will see that it has a branch to the left, then one to the right, then another on the left, which forks up and down. On the lower fork there is a leopard, and if you look over its back you will see the starling."

I heard them repeating my directions in low murmurs as they scanned with their binoculars. "Main trunk . . . branch left . . . branch right . . . branch left . . . oh my goodness, there really is a leopard!" said an unfamiliar voice. And I realized it was Rosemary.

"Yes dear, but you really must concentrate on the starling and make sure that the bugger was right with his identification," Basil admonished, already checking in his book.

I was unoffended and watched happily as Jamie and Jill both surreptitiously lowered their glasses to look at the beautiful cat. Many people come to Africa again and again without seeing a leopard, so when the starling took off, I sat there a little while longer before taking them back to camp.

At the airstrip, we all watched the Cessna arrive to take them away. "Thank you so much," said Jill. "It's been really great. Thanks so much," she repeated. As the plane drew to a halt and its propeller wound down, it was time for them to be awkward about tipping in the way that only the English can. Americans just shake your hand, slap you on the back, offer you a place to stay should you ever be in Idaho, and when you look down there is a bunch of green notes in your fist. The English, though, seem terribly embarrassed about the whole concept of money, so they either explain that they have left something with the manager back at camp or try to turn it into a formal ceremony with each delegate giving a speech. In this instance both Jamie and Jill continued their profuse thanks as they handed me an envelope with "just a little something" and explained that I must "understand it was just because they appreciated all I had done," and "wasn't that leopard marvelous" they finished before hastily adding, "but the birds were the best, thank you so very much."

Basil brusquely handed me an envelope, "Grand!" he said. And I would have loved to have believed that he was referring to how much was in the envelope as opposed to the quality of the experience, but I doubted it.

"Humph," I said, by way of thanks.

For no real reason I believe that it is bad luck to look at your tips until the plane is out of sight. So I drove all the way back to camp, stopping to look at a few things that interested me, which included plants, animals, and birds, before I opened the envelopes. Jamie and Jill had been generous to a point that would not embarrass anyone, and the envelope from Basil contained a single English pound.

Perhaps he had expected to see more and blamed me, which sometimes happens when you are a guide. Perhaps he just didn't like me. Or maybe, as he'd indicated with his very first, barely heard "humph," he was punishing me for being a fraud. For what he saw right away, and now I knew as well, was that I am a nature lover, maybe even a bird nerd, but I was not one of *those* people.

The Fool and the Snake

Paul knew a lot about snakes. Despite this he wasn't one of those creepy guys who likes reptiles because he couldn't make real friends. In fact he was one of the only safari guides I knew who had as much sex as people imagined the entire profession did. He had an easy coolness that I envied and at one point had attempted to emulate. Then people started asking me why I had become aloof and twitchy, so I stopped.

A few of our regular guides were sick, so Paul was helping us out. So was Eugene, yet another guide who usually did the overland journeys rather than be based in one place. While Paul was casually cool, Eugene was one of those people who irritated you, without you ever being able to say exactly why. His demeanor was like someone who was always a bit stoned, and he peppered his speech with surfer phrases like "bodacious" and "gnarly," which may have been more impressive if we weren't in a land-locked country.

Paul and I were at the bar, gathering some drinks for a party we had planned for that night. We had chosen a location at a water-hole a mile or so from camp, where we could be as raucous as we liked without fear of offending any tourists. We were enthusiastic that for once we might have something resembling a social life. ("We had big party recently," I would tell my city friends. "There must have been at least six of us!") Paul and I had already had a few beers and were getting merry with remarkable ease.

Eugene had escorted the last guests back to their rooms, and we could see his flashlight beam bobbing as he made his way back. Then it dipped, and he shouted out, "Hey Paul, what sort of snake is this?"

Then, "Errrrrrgh!"

It wasn't the right thing to do, but Paul and I burst out laughing at the sound. We quickly curtailed it, regathered our professionalism, and ran down to find Eugene, who was universally known as Genius precisely because he wasn't. He was clutching his thumb with a bead of blood just welling from its meat.

"What bit you? Was it an adder? Mamba? Cobra?" Paul asked, rapid-fire.

"Don't know," Genius moaned. There was silence for a moment, except for some whimpering from Genius.

"Then why'd you bloody pick it up?"

He didn't answer. He gave us a description of the snake, and Paul was convinced the culprit was a member of the burrowing adder family. Eugene moaned at the news. We looked in a book, and it said that necrosis from their bite was rare, so he would most likely *not* watch his thumb endure cell death and rot off, like he would have if a puff adder had bitten him. He moaned at this news as well, which seemed a bit rude, so we sent him off with two of the female camp managers, who seemed inexplicably impressed by his wound.

"Party's over," I said to Paul. "Let's call Maun." If Genius's injury had been life threatening, I wouldn't have minded the loss of a night's fun. If he had been a guest, I wouldn't have been as surprised by his foolishness. But the injury was nothing but painful, and Eugene was *staff*, so he should have known better. I was as cranky as the local porcupines when they couldn't get into our bins.

"Hmmph," grunted Paul, and I knew that he felt as I did.

Mustering sobriety, Paul and I radioed on the emergency channel to Maun. In cases of such an event, the local head of our company slept with a radio in his room, and we had a nurse on staff who could be contacted at all hours. We told them we had a snakebite.

"Guest or staff?" our boss Alan asked. I knew if we said guest, he'd moan too. We told him staff.

"Who is it?" the nurse asked.

"Genius."

"Damn fool. Did it get him on the foot?" Alan asked.

"No. Hand. He picked it up."

Alan swore. Anyone who handles snakes knows there are two ways to pick them up. You can either use an over-and-under grip on the head or grab it right at the neck on either side. Anyone who has this base knowledge is aware that this works with every snake in the world, except for a peculiar few in Africa—the burrowing adders. Their fangs are hinged, and they can flick them sideways and scratch you with one no matter which way you are holding them. They are generally acknowledged as the only snakes in the world that we have no safe way of handling. Sensible people do not, out of idle curiosity, pick them up.

"Well he can pay for the plane we'll have to send in the

morning," our boss muttered. The nurse came over the radio and instructed that he should be watched all night. Paul and I made a plan.

We'd still have the party! We had to stay up anyway, so we'd have it around Eugene's bed! Perfect! We carried the beers, gin, and whiskey in a cooler back to his tent, dragged in some chairs, and turned up music loud enough to drown out his moaning but not so loud as to wake the guests.

Eugene moaned erratically, and I realized it corresponded directly to the distance that either of his "nurses" got from him. While I had no doubt he was in pain, I was extremely skeptical that he would die without one of the girls stroking his brow with a wet cloth, something that he had intimated. Paul and I still attempted to make a night of it, though we felt somewhat irked by all the attention the girls gave him.

Later in the night, Paul mellowed somewhat in his feelings. He sat on the edge of the bed, swaying noticeably from his drunkenness, and Genius wailed, a refreshingly new sound after hours of feeble moans.

"He doesn't think you're pretty," I told Paul.

"Wassa matter?" Paul slurred. "Your hand hurts?"

"Ye-es!" Eugene gasped. Then he added, "You're sitting on it!"

Soon after, we began to drop off to sleep, some making it back to their tents and others sleeping where they fell. Camp life resumed at dawn as it always did, whether we were hungover or not. Eugene's hand had taken on some remarkably pretty coloration in the night, and his fingers were much larger than they should have been, but otherwise he was absolutely fine. We were unapologetic for having had fun while Genius writhed, and he showed no remorse for almost putting an end to it.

We flew Genius out that morning. Some guests left, and some more arrived. I bumbled through my afternoon drive, then sat sleepily through the evening meal. As it ended and Paul and I escorted the last guests to their rooms, scanning the surrounding bush for glinting eyes, I asked him a question.

"Want to grab a drink?"

"No." Bushes nearby rustled, but it was only a breeze. "Do you?"

"No." I shone my light around, picking up nothing but a spider's eyes glinting on the path. "Do you reckon Genius is alright?"

"Don't care." We were back on the deck now, and a hyena that had been sniffing the table scampered away. "Do you?"

I laughed, but said nothing, even though I did care. Eugene was a fool, but this was not a job for reasonable people. Our night of fun could have been curtailed just as easily by me getting trampled by an elephant or Paul being bitten by a guest or any one of the other guides who took risks every day for our own entertainment. So it was with guilt that I heard that Eugene had resigned and that he would never come back.

Maybe it was due to carelessness, or alcohol, or both, but for some reason Al didn't tie up his boat one night.

For two years it floated and bumped along the lazily flowing channels of the Okavango. Occasionally it was picked up by the winter floods and crossed submerged plains, sometimes settling there in summer, when the waters receded. I imagine it would have presented a strange sight to any of the light aircraft that ferry people around the Okavango, this little tin boat stranded in a grassland or bobbing along and alone between the hippos and the crocs.

Members of the Botswana Wildlife Department found the boat on one of the many patrols they make to catch poachers. The registration on the boat was still visible, and once Al heard his old vessel was tied up just outside Xaxaba, he asked Cliffy and me if we wanted to get it for him.

"Sure," said Cliffy.

"Sure," I repeated. But I had a question: "Where are we going with it?"

"Duba," Al said, which was the name of a camp he co-owned. The obvious question that I should have put to Cliffy next was, "Do you know the way?" The answer was particularly pertinent, since we had become lost on the two previous occasions that we had been in a boat together. And both times we had been in familiar territory. But I did not ask, as he seemed confident. And the next thing I knew, we were renting a motor for our trip. The Wildlife Department officials said the old motor had been stolen.

We took our motor and borrowed a dented cooking pot from some friends who were domesticated enough to own one. Then we bought countless packets of two-minute noodles and some beer and vodka and packed a first aid kit lest an accident while cooking the former should occur while under the influence of the latter.

As we were lashing down the motor in the tray of the vehicle we were going to set out in, a guide walked out from his room at our company plot. Unlike Cliffy, who trained guides, and me, being based in a camp full-time, Paul took long overland trips of a few weeks at a time. We had caught him between journeys.

"Hey Paul!" Cliffy hailed. "We're going to Xaxaba to get Al's boat, then taking it to Xigera, then on to Duba. We're just gonna camp on islands along the way. Wanna come?"

"I've got a group coming in three days," Paul replied. "Pity. It sounds like fun."

Cliffy told him that we would be in the bush for only two nights. He could fly out from Xigera or if we made good time, he could grab a Cessna out of Duba.

"Sure," Paul said. "If you're sure that I'll be back in three days."

"Sure," said Cliffy.

Sure.

A driver took us over sandy roads for many hours to the

wildlife camp, where we got our first look at the boat. To say someone with no imagination had designed it was an insult to designers. There was no design at all. It was a plain rectangle of chevronned metal, with four slab sides, about ten feet long by five feet wide. A reinforced section at one of the shorter sides supported the motor, but otherwise it was nothing more than an oversize sardine tin.

Showing the sense of style and understanding of design that we had, we all said, "Cool," and then attached the motor. Because it was getting dark, we set up our mosquito nets just outside the Wildlife Department's camp. We hadn't bothered with tents, and I was careful to place my net between Cliffy's and Paul's, figuring that if a hungry lion came by, it would eat one of them and be full by the time it got to me. If either of them noticed my scheme, or had even thought about it, they didn't say so.

When the morning light pierced my eyelids, I started to scratch. Mosquito nets can be as effective at trapping bugs as they are at keeping them out. And looking at the yellowed eyes of the officials, I knew malaria was in the air and hoped that I hadn't contracted it again in the night. It had been years since I had taken a pill but only months since my last bout of the disease. While a happy side effect had been a dramatic weight loss, I was looking forward to getting into true wilderness in our boat, away from any humanity and the diseases we carry. Even though I had lived in the bush for several years, it had been a long time since I had actually camped. Now we were heading into places unknown to any of us, and I couldn't think of anything better.

We puttered away from the camp and opened the motor. The boat wasn't very fast, but we didn't care. We took turns at the tiller, making our way to a camp run by a smaller safari company, where we wanted to ask for directional advice.

The camp's oldest guide, a venerable-looking man from the Bayei tribe, was brought to us. We made some bush tea and asked how long he had guided in the Delta. He sniffed and said through missing teeth that he had always been there. Many of his generation had spent time in the mines of Johannesburg, but he had always been a fisherman or guide, and he knew the waterways of the Okavango like few people ever could. He was a living map, more valuable than any paper. The waterways shifted in the delta, as new channels formed and old ones dried up. Only a man like this would have the experience to know where we were likely to find sufficient depth to maneuver a boat.

We told him that we planned on traveling to Xigera, and he nodded, noisily sucking on a grass stem as he did.

"When?" he asked.

We looked at each other, then back at him. "Today."

He raised an eyebrow, sucked on the grass, blew on his tea, and took a noisy, appreciative slurp. Shaking his head he told us that the floodwaters were going down and we would need to move fast but probably wouldn't make it anyway. "How big is your motor?" he asked.

"It's a twenty-five." We all knew this was not very big.

His other eyebrow came up, then both settled into a frown. "Your boat, it is pointy?" he made a triangular gesture with his hands that was far from describing the prow of our floating sardine tin.

"Er, no." At this news he puffed out his grass stem and gave us a contemptuous look.

"This boat, does it have a flat bottom?"

"Yes!" we answered in unison, delighted to give an answer that would please. His look changed from contemptuous to sympathetic, and like a father who allows his children some gentle knocks so they can learn life's lessons, he sent us off, giving us directions that quickly seemed meaningless once we were in the maze of channels and lagoons.

Our plan was to find one of the Okavango's main channels, called the Boro River, that flows right past Xigera. At Xigera we would be fed, maybe even have a shower, and then putter along to Duba. All we had to do now was find the Boro. We were determined to prove that the journey could be made in a square-fronted, under-powered vessel while the waters dropped.

At the very first fork in the channel after leaving the old man, we debated which way to go.

"Left," said Cliffy confidently. "That's the Boro." He looked to the right, and a frown flickered across his brow. "Maybe."

"Right," said Paul. I thought he was offering an opinion. Then he continued, "Let's decide this rationally. Who has a coin?"

"Wait. Look at the papyrus," I said, feeling proud of a deduction I was about to reveal. "The Boro flows all year round. Papyrus is growing on the channel to the right but not on the one to the left. There must be water in that channel all year round for it to grow—which makes it the Boro. We go right."

The two agreed with my line of argument, and we went right. What I had not factored in was that the channel on the left might be flowing strongly enough to sweep away any papyrus before it grew. The channel we took was not the Boro River. It was one of the many nameless waterways in the vast Okavango, and from the moment we pointed the square prow of the boat into it, we were lost.

■ ■

The first night, still confident that we were on the right channel or at least close to it, we found a small island to camp on. It was about fifty yards in diameter and, like many Okavango islands, a near-perfect circle. Salty sand covered the middle. From the sand grew a spiky grass that stabbed your feet as you walked over it, often drawing pinpricks of blood. On the edge of the sand grew clumps of palms. On the outer edge of the island, a variety of fruit trees grew, such as mangosteens and waterberries. We set up our mosquito nets, attaching them to low-growing branches, and built a fire to ward off any predator that might swim onto the island at night. Cat watchers from other parts of Africa might scoff at the idea of swimming lions, but anyone who has worked in the Okavango knows that a very big cat can be found on a very small island. We were on guard and quietly admitted to each other that we might have crossed the line between bravery and stupidity by not bringing a tent.

Despite our nerves we fell asleep remarkably early, the freshest of air helping us, aided by the last of the beer that we drank faster than we had planned. Soon a snuffling sound awoke me—the sound of a sizable animal—and I was thankful for my center position. Accompanying the snuffle was rhythmic thumping, fading and rising—the sound of drumming. For the first time ever in my years in Africa, I felt like I was in a Tarzan movie.

I peeled open an eyelid and watched the culprit as he snorted at us and stomped his feet. Islands like this one often have hollow patches where long-decayed trees once put down their roots. He was stomping on these hollow patches, running past us then around the palms that our head faced, tapping his feet, and then coming back to face us, stomping irritably again.

It was a porcupine—a big one. The African porcupine can weigh more than sixty pounds, and with its quills raised, as they were on this fellow, can reach an imposing three feet high. He was doing laps around us, a behavior you would expect from a caged animal. All night he ran, making further sleep an impossibility. I lay wondering why he was so possessed and came up with many theories that grew increasingly less likely in direct proportion to my level of fatigue. Ultimately the most realistic scenario that came to me was that he was marooned on the island when the floods came in. And because porcupines are one of the few animals in the Okavango that hasn't adapted to become a swimmer, he couldn't leave. This Robinson Crusoe of the rodent world may have been trying to get us off his island, or he may have been trying to communicate and make friends, turning us into his Man Friday, Saturday, and Sunday.

When the sky became gray, then pink, the porkie finished his last lap and dived into an unseen burrow somewhere under the palms. We stretched, scratched, cooked up some noodles on the embers of our fire, and set out again.

The channel was broad. And in the still morning air, the water was free of ripples as the sardine tin puttered along. Cliffy was convinced that we were not far from Xigera. I'd spent little time in the Xigera region, and so I was happy to go along with his assessment that we should be there sooner than we had expected.

"This channel curves just ahead, then we come out into an area with plains on either side, then we're only five minutes from the camp. We'll be in time for brunch!"

After two days of two-minute noodles, I looked forward to an omelet, so I happily swung the boat around the curve that Cliffy had predicted, but grew perplexed when the channel did not open into plains. Instead it grew tighter, the reeds and papyrus brushing the boat's sides.

Tighter and tighter it got, and now we knew why we needed the pointy prow the old man had spoken of. The boat's square end got jammed against the reeds, and the motor was not strong enough to move us forward unaided.

We convened. Cliffy was sure that we were still close, just not on the channel he had thought. Paul concurred, I said "Sure," and we decided to use the machetes we had brought to hack our way forward to the next open water, while one of us helped push from the back.

I volunteered to push while the others hacked, thinking I would avoid the inevitable blisters from the cheap plastic handles on the machetes. Instead, my first step revealed that I had the raw end of the deal. A tendril of aquatic grass with sharp, hairy fronds wrapped itself around my knee. It pulled tight as I stepped forward, and more tendrils found my other leg. It felt like I was being molested by an aggressive and spiny octopus, and every step drew the grip tighter. The leaves were little blades, and I suffered a thousand paper cuts as I pushed and heaved, dodging the spinning propeller that was only inches from my thighs.

"Get in," said Paul.

"Wha?" I had time to say, before Paul leaned over and hauled me in.

We had punched through the blockage and entered a lagoon, surely the home of at least one large crocodile. But it was not to protect me from this that Paul had pulled me in. Our arrival at the lagoon was greeted with a cacophony of snorts and bellows, followed by violent splashing and the rearing of enormous bodies. We drifted into the hippos, the propeller so clogged with grass it was barely effective. A bull hippo with a head broader than any of our shoulders opened his mouth, showing his chipped and yellow ivory spears, and charged toward us.

"Paddle!" Cliffy shouted. Paul and I set to with the machetes, using their blades as oars, as Cliffy eked what propulsion he could from the motor. We felt a bump, and the boat lifted but did not tip. If it had, we would not have lived for long. We powered through, a frenzied dragon boat team, until we were out of the lagoon and into the channel that fed it.

Now there were plains on either side of us, but Cliffy admitted that he really didn't know where we were. Neither did Paul, and I was equally clueless.

"Maybe we took the wrong fork, right at the start," I admitted quietly. The others said nothing, so I knew they agreed. "Should we go back and take the other one?" I asked. Paul has an ability to say multiple things with a single look, and he glanced in the direction we had come just as a hippo snorted. The decision was made. We pressed on, convinced that the Boro River must feed the channel we were on and that at some point they would link up. It was yet another decision that we would be able to laugh at later when we saw aerial photographs of the region we had been in. We were miles from anywhere with a name, miles from any village, miles from any safari camp, miles from help if we needed it.

We kept pushing forward, and the channel kept getting narrower and shallower. On occasion we would have to pull the boat through the lowest patches, and it wasn't necessary to point out that we were not on the Boro River. We decided that Paul would pull the boat forward while Cliffy would walk on foot east across the plains to look for deeper water. I walked west in search of the same.

I walked through lush green grass, cropped neat and short by zebra and wildebeest. In the distance impalas gave alarms and ran away, and some lechwe—another type of antelope—splashed through shallow water to avoid me. The scene was beautiful, and I stood for a moment before strolling to the only tree in the plain and climbing it.

I was watchful for snakes as I climbed, and wary of bees, but found none. Scanning the distance I could see a channel, but it was far, far away. We would not be able to carry the boat to it. I appreciated the view for a while longer, tracking a group of storks that were stabbing at fish caught in a pond, before looking back to see Paul straining along in front of the boat. I climbed down, scraping the front of my knees so they matched the abraded backs.

Back at the boat, Cliffy said he had also found a channel. This one, though, was reachable, as the eastern plain was still covered with shallow water. The flat-bottomed boat, once our weight was removed, could be coerced over it. We set to it, gently guiding the boat to a distant row of trees that indicated deep water. Wading along in ankle-deep water, we all agreed that lost or not it was one of the best adventures we had ever had. After some more splashing, Paul added that as much fun as he was having, he had to be back in Maun the next day to start a safari so maybe we should move faster.

We pushed harder and made it to the deep water. For the first time in hours, we moved with speed, the propeller free of debris and the water clear of obstacles. There was a sense of urgency but also incredible freedom. We whooped and laughed and drank vodka mixed with Okavango water and fruit-flavored rehydrating salts from the first aid kit.

Paul was at the tiller when we came around a curve that had a steep bank on our right. He quickly cut the motor and raised an eyebrow, which Cliffy and I understood to mean that we should be quiet and sit still. He squatted, so the highest point on the boat was the drum of fuel. Paul's outstretched finger indicated we should look ahead, and we saw a cheetah coming down to drink. It was intently checking for crocodiles, and we were close enough to see it hiss at the water before it noticed the odd lump of metal that was gently paddling toward it.

It jumped and turned a three-sixty in the air before launching itself back across the plain at freakish speed, not even stopping to look back. This was a cheetah that had either had bad experiences with a human or had never seen one before.

Paul powered up again, and we surged ahead, the square bow throwing a light spray. His face now had a look that said, "Okay, let's stop dicking around, find Xigera, and get a plane to take me to work." Cliffy and I were on leave, so we were in no such hurry. But we knew that our boss would hold us as responsible as Paul if eight tourists were left at Maun airport with nobody to guide them.

I looked at the banks of the channel we were traveling on,

and they were closer to the boat than when we had seen the cheetah. The water was shallower too, and I knew what this meant. Paul's pursed mouth told me he knew too, and soon the water was so shallow that he and Cliffy got out and I took my turn pulling the boat while they scouted for another channel. Cliffy went east, Paul went west, and I pulled straight ahead.

I was in a crucifix position, arms outstretched against the flat front of the boat. The channel was barely wide enough for the boat's passage but was still waist deep. At times I had to scrape the boat partially overland, my legs driving forward as my feet sank into the soft sand underneath, squelching back out. Despite the labor, I was enjoying myself. I knew for sure that this was a place where nobody had ever been.

I smiled at the sky. I smiled at the wide grassy plains that stretched treeless forever on either side of me. I smiled at the zebra that whistled and kicked the air in the distance. I smiled at the pied kingfisher that hovered and dropped for small fish in the channel ahead. And I even smiled as I stubbed my toe on a log and stumbled forward, the boat clanging into the back of my head.

I righted myself, took a step forward, and had an epiphany. The beauty of the scenery was defined by its lack of trees. There really shouldn't be a log here.

The log moved, I looked down, and my phobia came to life. I had walked the full length of a crocodile's tail and most of its back. My left foot was now between its shoulders, and I imagine it must have been thinking, "Well if you're idiot enough to walk into my mouth . . . "

With an athleticism I was unaware I possessed, I pulled down the front of the boat and hauled myself up, like a gymnast on the Roman rings, hooking my buttocks on the lip of the bow and doing half a backflip in. I landed on my head with a resounding "dong," but it was my strangled cry that drew Cliffy and Paul's attention, just in time to see the croc's tail flick as it headed for less busy waters.

"It's your turn to pull the bloody boat!" I shouted to whomever would listen from my upside-down position. But Cliffy had yet again found another channel.

"This is the Boro Rover!" Cliffy proclaimed, beaming. "I'm sure of it!"

Sure.

We again dragged the boat through shallow water cross-country and sped north once more. This was deep water, overhung with strangler figs that held the nests of fish eagles. The eyes of otters peered from tangled roots, and monitor lizards basked on the steep banks.

We spoke of eating one of the lizards, since we were out of noodles, but the place felt sacred, so we decided to go hungry and let the animals' first experience with man not be a predatory one.

Dusk came, and with it the last chance of finding Xigera that day. It was too risky to drive the boat at night through unfamiliar waters. A tree root might cut the boat open, or an unseen hippo could tip us in a panic. So we camped again, on a larger island this time—one that would be part of a forest when the waters receded some more.

We were more subdued around the fire than we had been the previous two nights. The waters were dropping faster than we had imagined, so we probably didn't have the option of going back the way we had come. The plains could be completely dry, and we would be stranded.

In the morning I went for a pee, moving away from the other two and relieving myself against a sizable patch of tall, dry grass that swayed like a wheat field. As I was finishing the grass rustled, and I imagined another porcupine running late in getting back to its burrow.

Instead a honey badger emerged, and I had never felt so vulnerable. Every guide has a fear of encountering a honey badger on foot because of the animal's penchant for genital mutilation. And now I was standing in front of one with my pants down, which was surely asking for it.

I knew it was one of the only animals that a human has a chance of outrunning, but it was not an option with my hips pinned by gaping canvas shorts. I cursed the difficult-to-fasten button fly as the badger stepped closer and sniffed my shin. He looked at me with no hostility, just curiosity, then trotted away. I slowly finished up and went back to Cliffy and Paul, who were busy hatching a plan.

"We're ditching the boat!" Cliffy announced. "And we're walking to Mombo!"

It was a great plan, I thought, but only if we knew which way to go to get there. I posited this and was told that since our original turn had been to the right, Xigera must have been to the left, and Mombo was by this reckoning just farther to the right. These were not bearings that would have pleased Magellan, I mused, but I was keen to give it a go anyway.

We left the boat wallowing in a lagoon, tied to a sturdy tree, and started our walk. We dropped the bright red fuel tank in the first open area we reached so that we could look for it later from a plane. All we carried were some water bottles, the first aid kit in case of accident or snakebite, and the machetes in case Cliffy was wrong and we decided to eat him.

None of us had serious doubts about our survival skills, and we knew that if we maintained a single direction we would eventually reach the end of the Delta. Once there, we could follow its fringe all the way around until we hit Maun. Then we could look for new jobs.

Paul was setting the pace, walking fast, somehow still believing that we might make it to Mombo early enough for him to get a flight to Maun in time to meet the three o'clock flight from Johannesburg and his guests. It was a ludicrous idea, and I stopped by the skull of a huge crocodile that littered the grass.

"Guys, are we just trying this because we don't want to admit defeat? If we really pushed it, don't you think we could make it back to Xaxaba in time for Paul to get out? I mean, if this guy couldn't make it," I tapped the skull with my foot, "how well are the three of us going to do out here?"

Paul's look said it all. We trudged back to the boat, turned it around, and let the current pick it up before starting the motor.

Our mood was defeated and our heads hung low, so it took a while for us to notice the strange way the water was acting in front of us. It bubbled—not just with ripples but with froth and flashes of silver. It was alive and moving toward us.

"Barbel run!" Cliffy shouted. The head of an enormous catfish emerged from the water, its mouth filled with minnows, then plunged back into the depths.

This was a phenomenon I had heard of but had never

witnessed. As the flood recedes, the millions of little fish who have hatched in the shallow plains swarm en masse back to the deep channels. Catfish—which in Africa are called barbel—mass into groups tens of yards long and rush into the minnows, gorging on the plentiful supply and making the water foam as it did now.

We cut the motor so we weren't chopping the fish up, and our world soon filled with the racket of hundreds of tails and fins slapping the tin as the barbel attacked.

Soon they passed, and we watched the slaughter continue upstream. Around us floated a few dead minnows, like the remnants of a great battle.

"I've never seen that before," I said. Neither had the others. Between us we had more than twenty years' experience in the bush, so seeing something new was unusual. We nodded at each other, acknowledging that this trip had been an experience, whether we had made it to Xigera or not.

One more hippo came at us on our trip downstream, but we easily outpaced him now that the current was pushing us. And soon we saw the distant camp that we had left three days earlier.

We left the boat at Xaxaba, and the three of us flew to Maun, picked up by a pilot friend who had just started arranging a search for us. Paul rushed to the plot, and after a quick shower and shave, met his guests, who will no doubt always tell of their adventurous ten-day African adventure, just as we would always speak of the three days we had spent lost on a boat.

The Conversation

The wildebeest had been dead for about two days and was starting to get a funky odor in the hot September sun. Armed with orange peel that I suggested my guests stuff in their nostrils, we sat and watched the lethargic lions as they ambled up, took a mouthful of flesh or two, then strolled back to the shade of the bush and flopped down, bellies bulging, doing little else except panting and farting.

My guests took their photos and made bathroom jokes, but didn't seem so offended by the stench that we needed to move on. The first two rows of seats held elderly couples from Europe, and in the back row sat a shy American man who was perhaps in his early forties. I had explained that because the rear seat sat behind the axle it was often the bounciest, and that for the sake of politeness people should rotate through it. He had insisted on taking it for every drive, though, as he didn't want the older people to feel any discomfort. For every drive, he sat quietly, nodding as I explained the behavior of animals and birds and where they all fit in the environment. He was clearly enjoying his safari, but he carried a melancholy with him that made me wonder if he was traveling alone because he had lost a partner. But I thought it impolite to ask.

The American was as quiet as ever as I explained that

despite the bulk of the prey, there would soon be little to show of its existence. The lions would eat the bulk of the meat, then hyenas would crack the bones for the nutritious marrow inside. Jackals would be next, accompanied by vultures. Even flesh-eating beetles would arrive, which would strip the tiniest scraps of gristle from whatever fragments remained.

"You could send in whatever forensic experts you wanted in a week or so, and there would be no evidence at all of this animal having been here. This is the best place in the world to commit a crime, if that's what you wanted to do." People laughed politely, but not too deep, lest any of the rancid air get into their mouths.

■ ■

We returned to camp for brunch, which was devoured voraciously despite earlier claims in the stench that nobody was ever going to eat again. I ate just as heartily, excused myself, and started walking back to my vehicle. I was going to drive it to the back of camp to hose down, but in the turning circle the shy American stalked me and made his approach.

"That sure was funny what you said back there," he laughed, a strangely nervous-sounding laugh for someone who was paying a compliment.

"Thank you," I said. "But which thing?" I thought I said a lot of funny things, though my colleagues constantly assured me that I did not.

"About being able to get away with murder out here." He wiped perspiration from his face. It was winter. "Yeah . . . really funny. And interesting."

"Yeah!" I said, enthusiastically. "You could do pretty much anything. The cops are a hundred miles away, and I don't think they're that competent anyway. In fact, if you did it somewhere like Zimbabwe, you could just pay the cops not to investigate. It would make a great thriller. Are you a writer?" I'd been rambling on and by the look on his face realized that no, he wasn't a writer, which made me seriously question why he wanted to know how to get away with murder.

The world crashed back. This wasn't happening, I thought, feeling a cocktail of outrage and reptilian fascination with this man who up until now I had slightly pitied. I should find a way to walk away, I thought, but banged my shin on the step as I tried to casually get into the vehicle.

"Bugger," I said. "Klutz. That's me. You wouldn't want me handling anything serious." I thought this was a genius strategy of disentanglement. I really didn't want to hear who this man planned on introducing to the African food chain, and I wondered exactly which authorities I should contact.

"Ha, ha, ha," the man laughed again, which was inappropriate since I had just hurt myself and we were talking about murder. At least I thought we were, but I really didn't know. Maybe he was just trying to make friends. The most awkward silence I have ever endured followed, until I again tried to swing myself into the Land Rover and banged my shin in the same place.

He didn't laugh this time, and I certainly didn't either. I just clutched my injured limb and contemplated feeding whomever I had inherited my uncoordinated genes from to an animal as well.

"It wouldn't really work," I said.

"Why not?" He looked crestfallen.

"Tracks," I said this as if it was self-explanatory, just to make him squirm.

"Tracks?"

"When an animal kills another, they leave tracks. Two sets in, bad smell in the middle, one set out. It's not forensics, but it's still evidence." I watched him nod as he digested this, and he looked defeated.

"Okay," he said. "Okay," softer this time, and his voice hitched as if he was heartbroken. I was intrigued now as well as repelled, and was desperate to know who in his life had driven him to ask such questions. Or was he playing with me?

"There's no such thing as a perfect murder." I said. "There's nothing perfect about killing someone."

"Oh yes, of course," he said, looking suddenly lost, embarrassed, and incredibly lonely. "I was just asking because . . . it was interesting."

I still wasn't sure why he was asking. I looked to see if one of the guides or managers were nearby, grinning at a prank they had played, but we were alone. I wanted to question him now, to know for sure, but was flustered and didn't know where to begin.

So I left it where it stood, and to this day pray that he did the same.

A Guide Dies

Rantaung Rantaung had exuberantly doubled up on a name ("Call me Double R," he would say to guests, smiling enormously, "just like Rolls Royce!"), so it was perhaps appropriate that he should have two deaths.

But before he died, he was a guide at Mombo. And before that, he'd had to apply not just for the job, but to join the gang.

We'd had a quick turnover of guides, with a number of unsatisfactory applicants briefly filling the vacant position. One candidate, to the horror of his guests, took great and perverse delight in running over slow-moving tortoises, even veering off the tracks to pursue them. Another guide was from Gaborone, the capital city, and spoke flawless English in a seductive, mellifluous voice that would have charmed birds from the trees if he chose to use it that way—but he did not, and that was his problem. He showed his guests no animals because he was absolutely petrified of wildlife and turned his vehicle and fled at even inoffensive creatures like zebras and warthogs. The third was an accomplished tracker, a competent driver, and a reasonable communicator, but he was inexcusably gross, picking his nose ceaselessly and farting his way through meals. The management had quickly ended the probationary period of all three and approached a guide they had both worked with at another camp.

I sincerely hoped he would be up to par. There were now only three guides at Mombo, which meant that we rarely had any sort of break in the seven-day-a-week, three-month-long stints that we worked before taking leave. I was exhausted and yearned for at least one morning that I didn't need to wake at five o'clock. So it was with some selfish hope that I drove to the dusty airstrip one day to pick up Rantaung, the next candidate.

On the road to the airstrip, you pass a perfectly proportioned baobab tree. Its base is wide enough that an elephant could hide behind it if the urge ever overtook one, and its top tapers to form a perfect bottle shape. The baobab is remarkable, beautiful, and the perfect place for a nap if a plane is ever late. A guest of mine with the odd hobby of dendrochronology had estimated its age at roughly one and a half thousand years, and I loved to imagine the things the tree would have seen—the lions, elephants, the now extinct rhinos, and the years when humans moved in as cattle herders, were driven out by tsetse flies, then returned as tourists.

Baobabs have a magic about them, so the tree makes the ideal place for an informal church. Every Saturday night the staff members who are devotees of the Zionist Christian Church attend a service there. These are presided over by one of the guides, whose name is Baikego Setlabosha. Since that proves a bit of a mouthful, he is known as BK, even to the staff who come from his village. He was my best friend among the guides and had a taught me most of what I knew about finding animals. On the day I was to pick up Rantaung, he was also at the airstrip, waiting for guests of his own.

BK looked as tired as I felt, but I knew he would not show any fatigue to his guests. He was a complete professional in his work, and I envied him for the unaffected air of contentment he radiated.

Rantaung's energy only highlighted our fatigue when the plane disgorged its passengers. He bustled out first, talking loudly and excitedly to the guests. He expressively waved his skinny arms to guide the tourists as they negotiated themselves past the struts and braces that make light aircraft so much fun to enter and exit, and then he ran beaming to me and BK. He quickly pumped our hands and introduced himself to me, explaining that his first and last names were the same, so they were easy to remember. He gave BK a hug, and I saw the badge on his shirt that signified he was a member of BK's church.

The guests had finally unfurled their limbs from inside the fuselage, and BK and I shook their hands and took their luggage to the vehicles. Rantaung assisted me, then hopped into the passenger seat of my vehicle, grinning like he had won a prize for being first out of the plane. I soon realized that a smile was his default position.

The couple who had been allocated to me were nondescript Midwesterners, but I was delighted to overhear the way BK's guests announced themselves. "Bob Johnson! Houston! Texas! And this is my wife, Mary!" The man thrust his hand out as he barked each word. It had always struck me as peculiar when people who were introducing themselves gave their name and where they were from, like rank and number. But it was that they were from Texas that made me so happy. When BK or I were guiding people from Texas, the game was on.

BK gave his name (but did not add, "Jao Village. Northern Botswana.") and then said, "... and this is my son, Peter."

I saw the Texans look at me, and their smiles faltered. The Midwesterners gasped. Rantaung just smiled at everyone, as if the announcement was exactly what he had been expecting. The shaking of hands carried on, the arrivals all glancing at each other askance, wondering if they had heard correctly. The reason for their perplexity is that BK and I could not look less like father and son. For a start he is only ten years older than me, and physically we are quite different. While I am not tall, BK is at least a head below me and is far more solidly built. His hair is tightly curled, whereas mine, whenever it emerges from under a hat, is straight to the point of being lank.

The most distinguishing difference, though, is that BK is dark skinned, and I am not. In fact I am so pale that I like to say that I can't sleep naked, because I am kept awake by moths bumping into my backside, mistaking it for the luminous moon. It is this blanched appearance that made people so sure that they must have misheard BK, and why it was so much fun for me to shout as I drove away, "See you back at camp . . . Dad."

Rantaung didn't comment, and I asked him if he owned any cattle and congratulated him when he said he did. This is the polite way to meet a man in Botswana. I then asked my guests if they had enjoyed the camp they had just come from, what they hoped to see, and if they had been to Africa before—a fairly standard icebreaker. Throughout the back and forth I could feel the burning urge they had to ask about my relationship with BK. If they had come right out and asked if he was my father, I would have answered honestly. "Naah . . . that's just a game we play with Texans."

If they asked why we chose Texans, I would answer just as honestly that there was no real reason. It was just fun.

Once we arrived in camp, the guests were handed cool drinks and cloths to wipe the dust from their faces. The arrivals eyed me almost warily, assessing my features. Then one of the Texans asked if BK was really my father.

"Oh yes," I said, "but my mother was Swedish, which is like pouring bleach over your DNA. That's why I'm so white."

"Oh," said the Texans, still not convinced.

"But there was a problem." It was Rantaung, somehow picking up on the script without ever having been told about it. "Our cattle, which are like money to us here in Botswana, were afraid of him because he is so bright he hurts their eyes, so we had to send him all the way to Australia. That is why he talks in such a funny way."

" . . . and I only came back so I could learn the way of the bush from my father." I nodded at BK, "and my uncles." Here I nodded at Julius (the other permanent guide) and at Rantaung. He was, in my mind, now part of the gang.

■ ■

Later I spoke with Grant and Chris and told them I liked Rantaung and asked if he would be offered the job full-time.

"Probably. For as long as we've got him." They paused,

and I must have looked quizzical, because they added, "He used to be fat."

"Oh," I said, immediately comprehending. In Africa it is no cause for celebration if someone has lost a lot of weight. The usual cause is an illness such as malaria. Malaria strips meat from your bones faster than a butcher can, but since your appetite returns before your energy, the weight usually piles straight back on. If the fat doesn't come back, it usually indicates an even more serious illness.

At this stage I hadn't known anyone who had died from AIDS, although the statistics insisted that I must know a lot of people who were infected. One in three of the people whom I worked with were likely to be HIV-positive. But despite the never-ending parade of funerals that could be seen in Maun, the staff just didn't seem to get sick. An AIDS specialist had told me not to be overly hopeful about this, as part of the pay we received was in the form of three meals a day. So compared to a town dweller, we had a healthy lifestyle, which would for a while stave off the sort of ill-nesses that will ultimately kill a person with AIDS.

Rantaung got the job, and got the meals, but put on no weight. As I had never known him when he was bulky, nothing seemed untoward, and his sense of humor was certainly in robust health. It was Rantaung's special talent that he could make painfully bad jokes ("See that over there! A rock with legs! Oh no, it's an elephant!" was a standard), but tell them with such enthusiasm and laugh so uproariously at his own wit, that people couldn't help but join in.

Now, we all had our places in the gang. I spoke the best English and had the greatest book knowledge. This was counterpointed by BK's astonishing ability to find animals that no text or school could teach. He had grown up hunting for food with his father and could spot a leopard in a tree that was miles from the track. His calm demeanor also inspired confidence in his guests. Once, midway through a drive, he casually radioed me, told me where he was, asked if I was nearby, then mentioned offhandedly that his vehicle was on fire and he would like a lift back to camp. He was cool in the true sense of the word.

Julius was the greatest seducer of tips. Our salaries were minimal, and it was gratuities that really paid for whatever lives we led when on leave. Julius had a family to support, something he could casually insert into the most unrelated of topics without it being obvious that he was fishing. " . . . And do you have children?" his guests would ask. "Oh yes, I have six!" he would answer, or sometimes, seven, eight, or twelve. " . . . And do they go to school?" was the standard reply from the guests. "Only half of them. I want to send them all, but it is so expensive! So some must stay at home and help their mother plant the maize." You could almost hear the wallets falling open, and I was astonished at some of the fat, book-size envelopes I saw him receive from departing clients at the airstrip. He would have done well even without this trick, because he was an excellent guide, with a knack for knowing which way an animal would turn. He was always right at the spot where the lions brought something down, unerringly knowing which way their prey would flee. His other knack was for naming people. But even though we had worked together for a few years, it was Rantaung who gave me my second African name and my first in Botswana.

One morning as I worked on a Land Rover, he walked by,

looked at me, and burst out laughing. I quickly checked myself over and saw nothing untoward, except my patchy sunburn. I was out of uniform and wearing only shorts, exhibiting the unusual red bands that had come from driving around in the sun all day. My legs were white from the foot to the knee, then brown from there to the thigh. My nether region, belly, back, and chest were as pale as a fish's underside from being covered by clothing. The white stopped at the neckline, though, where there was a triangular patch at the top of my chest that spread onto my face. This region was an alarming burnt chestnut color. The same tint appeared again halfway down my biceps and ended at my fingers.

"You look like a Lehututu!" Rantaung burst out, and some other staff, who up until now had treated my odd markings as no more unusual than anything else about me, all joined in the laughter.

Lehututu is the Setswana name for a bird, which in English is called the ground hornbill. The Setswana name perfectly represents its deep, haunting call, which carries across the plains: "Le—hu—tu! Tu—tu!" It is turkey size and pitch-black in plumage, unless it shakes a tail feather at you. These feathers are as white as my rump, but I doubted Rantaung could have any idea how pallid that was. The parallel Rantaung had drawn was based on the hornbill's most distinctive feature: Its face and neck, in stark contrast to its pitch-black plumage, are the lurid red of a streetwalker's lipstick. Catching a glance of myself in the wing mirror, I had to admit he had a point.

From that point on, whenever he called me on the radio, that was the only name he used. Like a gang, we all had our names now—Rantaung was Double R, Julius was Galloping Horse (a name of his own choosing, and he became very grumpy whenever we altered it to Galloping Tortoise), and BK, perhaps due to his palpable dignity, just stayed BK.

For about a year we were a stable guiding group and found a working rhythm that we had lacked up until Rantaung had arrived. We learned from each other, honed the games we played with tourists, and reached the point that we could tease each other about skin color without worrying about offense. BK could claim the darkest skin and would mock Julius for his lighter tone, suggesting that somewhere in his heritage there was a Dutchman. Julius would in turn say that once all my freckles had joined together, I might actually start looking like BK's son. I would offer them all sunscreen at the start of each drive, to the bemusement of the guests, and Rantaung would make a show of lathering himself, then claim that he felt different now that he was white. He would look at the guests and say, "But to be like them I need more money! You need money to be fat like that!" I knew that all the money in the world wouldn't make Rantaung fat and would quickly scan the faces of BK and Julius after such a comment. I wanted to see if they were reserved in their laughter, but they would be openly guffawing, so I would join in as much as I could.

■ ■

The guides also took turns trying to teach me Setswana, which I had struggled with from the moment I arrived in the country. BK taught me some phrases, but when I tried them out on Rantaung, he just laughed and said, "That's not Setswana! He taught you Bayei! I'll have to teach you real Setswana, or you'll end out talking like a monkey!" Bayei was the name of BK's tribe and its language, which apparently Rantaung thought inferior to his. So Rantaung taught me some words, which Julius promptly told me were not Setswana either, but Hambakushu. Julius then gave me some words of Herero, even though he insisted they were part of the national language. And in the end I came to think that we all got on so well because nobody understood anyone else.

Most of the time we all spoke English with each other, talking about where the animals were, where they would most likely have gone since we last saw them, which lions were expecting cubs, and who would be the first to find them. We spoke of people—whose guests were good, and bad; and we complained about the managers. The others would usually complain about all white people, then add, "But not you . . . you're not white. You're a Lehututu." One thing we did not speak about was Rantaung's clearly failing health.

One morning after a drive, some of Rantaung's guests asked to change vehicles. This happened on occasion to all guides, because nobody can be expected to get on with everybody, but it is always a blow to the guide's pride. The guests complained that he spent too much time away from the vehicle tracking the animals. It struck me as strange, as the wildlife is so dense at Mombo that we rarely left our vehicles for long. Then Chris explained it to me: "He's going off into the bush to be sick."

Shortly after that he went into town to see a doctor, and I didn't expect to see him again. I didn't sleep that night, and by the look of it the next morning neither had BK or Julius. We waited for word of his condition, and waited some more. Then, to our surprise, three weeks later he came back, looking gaunt and wasted but smiling as much as ever.

"Hey Lehututu!" he shouted when he saw me. "You're fat! Nice!"

In Botswana saying someone is fat is a compliment, as it represents prosperity. There was no way I could return the favor, though, as it would be so patently untrue and only serve to point out that he was dying.

"Good to see you, Rolls Royce," I said instead.

He lasted another month, then went back into town "for some tests." Within two weeks one of our staff went to visit him and his family and was told that he had died moments before. Grant took the radio call and let us all know. The kitchen and laundry staff burst into wailing ululations, and the men looked down at their shoes and the dust that was slowly speckling with tears.

The wailing carried on for hours, an eerie sound drifting on the wind from the little village where the staff lived. A guest asked me what it was, and I told him that a friend, Rantaung, had died. My voice hitched as I said his name, but I held my lip firm and changed the subject. The Africans keened, a sound with no words that said everything, and I wondered if I would feel any better if I was with them and let go of the grief. For once I felt separate from the other guides, my Western sensibilities not allowing me to wail. In the village I would only make them feel uncomfortable, and I didn't want to do that. So I sat, tense, in my tent, trying to block the sounds from outside and waited for the afternoon drive to distract me.

Before the day was out, word came through the radio that Rantaung was still alive. He had collapsed, and his family had mistaken it for death. It seemed strangely cruel, because for me it was the fulfillment of a long-held wish. When my mother died, I would have given anything, anything at all, to have her back. I craved the news of some mistake, that through a miracle she was alive again. I have felt the same way about every other friend or acquaintance that has been lost. But when I learned that Rantaung still lived, it only seemed like a blow. It was a postponement, not a reprieve, and the word came within a week that this time he was dead for sure.

BK invited me to a service he was leading for Rantaung under the baobab tree on the way to the airstrip, and I gratefully accepted. From a distance the scene would have looked pagan—a fire, a leafless tree, and the dancing forms of dark-skinned people with one hunched white figure among them—but it was the most sacred experience of my life.

The next day I took a long walk, away from the camp and its memories, into the calming bush. I found an old snare, set by some long-departed poacher and probably forgotten. The snare was still killing, though, for it contained the carcass of an impala whose head and foreleg had been trapped through the cruel wire loop. Hyenas had eaten it, maybe while still alive.

I cut the carcass free and cried for the first time since learning of Rantaung's two deaths. I felt surrounded by senselessness. I twisted the wire angrily in my hands, trying to hurt it and drive the question I had from my mind.

For it is a terrible thing to wonder: Which of my friends is next?

A Night in the Madgkadigkadi

Shortly after I drowned two vehicles in the space of a month, my boss, Alan, asked me to do something for him. Even if I hadn't felt grateful for continued employment, I probably would have said yes. No matter how many elephants I have stood up to, I am easily bullied by people.

He'd heard I was going to Johannesburg for a few days and wanted me to bring something with me when I flew back.

"Sure," I said, imagining a spare part or a decoration for one of the camps that was too delicate to put in a truck.

Instead, it *was* a truck.

Sort of.

A mechanic with a touch of Frankenstein syndrome had taken one of our old Land Rovers and chopped into its already abused panels, cutting away everything but the cab section. On the bare chassis at the back, he had put a horseshoe-shaped attachment that you see on big rigs, and to this he attached a trailer, about the length of a city bus, making a mini-semitrailer. This is what my boss wanted me to bring back.

"Er, I don't think that's going to fit in my luggage. Air Botswana can be pretty strict about that."

"I've canceled your ticket," he said. Since the company had

booked it for me, I knew he was probably telling the truth. "Enjoy your drive," he added, knowing I wouldn't.

I'm sure this was his revenge for my expensive mistakes. He'd made me drive an open vehicle once before, for the same thousand-mile Kalahari-crossing trip, and I had loudly declared that I would never do it again—that I would only fly from Johannesburg to Maun from now on. The drive was infamous for its dangers, which came in unexpected ways. The first was monotony. The unvarying open landscape that was at first breathtaking eventually became skull-numbingly boring and could lull even the most nervous driver into a sense of security, even sleep. This left drivers likely to encounter, and in a bad way, one of Botswana's most unexpectedly dangerous animals—the donkey. But I was in no position to refuse. Alan gave me his wolfish grin, then a set of keys.

"Keep the receipts for any fuel you need. And don't forget to fill up in Nata." And with that I was on my own, except for the contraption that was mine for the two days the drive should take if I drove at a sane speed.

I'd had a bit too much fun the night before and had gotten less than three hours' sleep, and my head was telling me that the sun was way too bright and penetrating to begin the journey. It was also midday. The crossing over the Limpopo River between South Africa and Botswana closed at six o'clock, and I had no idea whether or not the odd-looking vehicle would be fast enough to make the journey before the border shut. Common sense and my hangover told me to wait a day. But if I had listened to those forces throughout my life, I'd be a lawyer in Sydney.

So I set off and noticed straight away that the fuel gauge didn't work. I swung into the first service station I saw, and I almost rolled the truck. I'd never driven an articulated vehicle before, and I was not used to the way it handled. No swinging, I thought to myself. I gathered control—and my nerves—and looked to see on which side the filler hole was, but I quickly realized that I had no side mirrors. Johannesburg drivers have been known to open fire for the most minor of errors, so I nervously held up traffic as I ran around the vehicle and found the filler hole, which the mechanic had moved so it was down low and involved acrobatics to get the nozzle into. I hastily climbed back in, overshot the pump, almost knocked it over when I tried to back up and the trailer jackknifed, and then went in to pay. I was convinced everybody was staring at me thinking, "What an idiot. Let's shoot him in case he breeds."

As I took out my wallet, I realized I had very few rand on me. I'd blown a lot of cash the night before, and there was no way this place was going to accept Botswana pula. I had just enough to pay for the diesel I'd put in and to buy some snacks and six locally concocted energy drinks I figured would assist me through my hangover. They promised caffeine, guarana, bull-testicle extract, and a variety of complex chemicals at levels that I imagined would keep me hopping for a month.

Hanging above the indifferent man who served me (who managed the entire transaction with one hand while the other picked his nose) were a variety of tools such as jacks and wheel wrenches, which gave me pause. I went back to the rig and looked everywhere I could think of, turning up a wheel wrench but no jack. I tested the wrench on the front wheel, and it fit. I figured I could improvise on the jack if I needed to. Poor judgment was having a field day in my aching head.

I pulled out, the vehicle shuddering and groaning as it drove off. The fuel gauge still read zero, stuffing was missing from the passenger seat and a cruel-looking spring stuck out, a dark cavity took the place of the radio, and there was no air-conditioning, which was really of no importance because there were no windows. Instead the top of the door had a piece of wood screwed into it, which made a handy place to rest my elbow so I could start working on a sunburn.

I quickly whipped my arm in when I realized I needed both hands, as the power steering was a random thing and only worked when I was on a straight road. This vehicle wanted to punish whomever drove it for the strange things that had been done to its rear end. I tend to give human characteristics to inanimate objects—even name them—and ignore how ridiculous it is to believe that a vehicle doesn't like you. As the rig crabbed around the first corner, terrifying me and the two drivers it almost wiped out, I named it Dick.

Dick had many strange habits. There was his reluctance to move forward, his disturbing willingness to go sideways, his negligible brakes, and his squeaks, rattles, and groans that would shame a brothel's bed. Despite all this, Dick and I made good time to the border, although I had no way of knowing that until I got there. I don't wear a watch, and Dick's speedometer, not surprisingly, didn't work. Along the way, with nobody to talk to, repetitive landscape, and perhaps a touch of OCD, I drank three of the energy drinks. I'd bought only junk food at the store, as it was heavily packaged against the cashier's snot-encrusted fingers. With this cocktail of sugar, salt, and bull juice in my system, I crossed the border and drove into the open, flat lands of the Kalahari.

The only thing that seemed to work on Dick was the accelerator, although at high speed he developed a disconcerting wobble. I kept it pushed, glad that Botswana has no hills. We flew past wind-whipped thorn trees, startling weaver birds from their nests and spitting sand from our tires. I braked for chameleons as they made their wavering way across the road, but I would not touch the middle pedal for anything else, easing off the speed only when I passed through the occasional heat-baked village. Dust billowed across the landscape and through the place where Dick's windows should have been, coating my teeth with a gritty paste I washed down with more energy drink.

The concoctions now made up a large percentage of my bloodstream. Buzzed, I started singing, probably scaring more birds and definitely making the chameleons abandon their usual cautious step in order to scurry from my offensive tonsils. I laughed at how my bad singing voice (which sounded "like a constipated seagull," my father had once told me) was made even worse by the dust and a piece of corn chip stuck in my throat. I laughed, then guffawed, then shouted out something like, "Whooooooeeeee!" into the vast silence, and I knew that Dick was being driven by someone who was a bit nuts. Should probably ease off the energy drinks, I thought, glancing at the last can that was heating up on the torn seat beside me. I swigged it down anyway, thinking it would be no good later when the sugars were cooked. It would have cooled soon enough, though, as the sun had dipped, turning the dust storms bubblegum pink and putting a cool tinge on the air that whipped through the cab.

The combination of cold, sugar, and whatever stimulants they allow in African energy drinks kept me shivering and clenching and releasing my jaw, chewing furiously at the last of my snacks. I wanted to make it to Nata by full dark, so I could spend the night there before crossing the world's largest salt pans. I wasn't going to make it.

I contemplated pulling over and snoozing beside the road, but the drinks had me wired and I had set a goal for Dick and myself, so we carried on, disregarding the dangers of night driving in Botswana. As it grew darker, I flicked Dick's switches until lights dimly appeared at slightly crazy angles ahead of us. Only one high beam worked, and it seemed to be scanning for helicopters. This was a problem, because at night on this road, I needed to keep both eyes fully peeled and my wired senses alert for donkeys.

In the flat plains during the day, I had found it easy to see the donkeys that lingered on the outskirts of some of the villages I had passed. Many of them were hobbled by the villagers, their front legs tied together to keep them wandering too far. I knew this would make them slower to get off the road if they saw Dick coming. I also knew that night was when they came onto the road for the warmth it radiated, and they were near impossible to spot on the unilluminated tar. I doubted that wobbly old Dick could stop in time if one stepped out in front of us. After diseases like malaria and HIV, collisions with donkeys are one of the leading causes of death in Botswana, so I took their threat seriously, gnashing away with caffeine-fueled, donkey-defying intensity.

I powered on through the Kalahari night, the occasional yelp of a jackal coming on the wind. At one point an ostrich careened wildly in front of me before dashing into the darkness. I laughed long and hard at his pumping and enormous drumsticks. I knew all the stimulants were still in my system and that I wasn't quite myself. I sang, chuckled, watched for donkeys, and acknowledged that despite my thumping pulse, I was skull-crushingly bored.

Dick gave a cough and we lurched, the steering wheel jiggling in my already shaking hands. I looked futilely at the fuel gauge. I'd filled up at the border and had figured I would make it to Nata easily. Dick gave yet another belch and jerked so violently that I was sure a donkey had just died beneath us. But we had not hit any equids, and we spluttered along, me patting Dick's dash, giving encouragement, telling him he was a good mini-semitrailer. I prayed that it was only dirty fuel that was making him a bit sick and not an absence of fuel altogether, and my calls were answered. We rolled into Nata just after eleven o'clock at night, the Kalahari stretch of our trip having taken just over ten hours. I was exhausted but knew that I wasn't going to sleep anytime soon. Instead of going straight to the campsite where I planned on staying (primarily because in the entire town, which was about fifty yards by fifty yards, it was the only option), I went straight to the diesel pump, which surprisingly was still open. Later I would wish that it hadn't been.

Astonishingly the person serving me was also excavating his nostrils, and I asked if he had any family working in the industry across the border. I had asked just to hear another voice, but he only shook his head in the negative. So I paid up, looked again at the collection of jacks, wheel wrenches, and other paraphernalia that I was too mechanically ignorant to identify, and wandered back to Dick, who sat ticking in the night air. I washed off the crust of bugs that had formed on his windshield, then used some more water to clean them away from his radiator as well, because the temperature gauge didn't work, and he may have been overheating. Across the road, the campsite's lit sign was attracting its own swarm of bugs. I knew there would be a tent that I could stay in and a bar where backpackers passing through would be sitting. Even though talking to strangers was what I did for a living, I'm still too shy to approach unfamiliar people without a good reason, and the thought of being among them made me feel more lonely than I would have been if I stuck with Dick. I was exhausted but knew that Maun, where I had friends and a place to stay, was only three or four hours across the Madgkadigkadi Pans. Dick ticked, I decided, and we went into the night, leaving Nata behind.

The Madgkadigkadi Pans would not seem unfamiliar to anyone from Bonneville, Utah, but they are even larger and flatter and have no human habitation within them. Donkeys were no longer a factor, as the land can sustain no villages. The whole huge area, many hundreds of miles across, is a national park with the one ribbon of road that cuts through it. In summer, when it rains, the shallow water fills with flamingoes. But it was still dry and all that would be around would be desert-dwelling antelope such as springbok and oryx and the predators they attracted. My friends, Richard and Rebecca, had seen a leopard the last time they had driven this road at night, and I knew others who had seen lions and cheetahs. Most people loathed the monotony of the dead straight road, unvarying landscape, and pervading dust after they had been through it only once, but the anticipation of what I might see always made me enjoy the drive.

I put my foot flat and we cruised at Dick's top speed, the measure of which was still a mystery to me. The air had cooled some more and carried the scent of wild sage, one of the few plants that could grow here. The lights illuminated a span of nothingness unequalled in the world. There was just road, dust, and cool night air. I hummed and felt my eyes grow heavy. We swayed to the middle of the road.

No.

I had to stay awake.

I had no idea how long I had been driving or how far I had to go.

I was out of drinks and had come to the conclusion that they only kept you from sleeping anyway; they didn't make you any more alert. The road swished under the tires, an insidious lullaby. "Maybe I should pull off the road, and nap," I said out loud, to see if speaking woke me up. But the road was built high, so it didn't wash away on the few occasions that rain fell. I wasn't sure that if I took Dick into the soft verge that I would ever be able to drag his sluggardly rear half back onto the tar.

Stay awake.

Stay awake.

Stay awake.

Stay awake.

Boom.

Dick yawed, the wheel twisting hard enough to sprain my wrist. We whipped right, and I had time to think "blowout" before I saw the verge come rushing at us. At this speed, at this angle, if we went off the twelve-inch drop, I would die, and I doubted that Dick would make it either. There were no seatbelts, and the violence of the swerve had thrown me almost to the passenger seat. I used my weight to drag the wheel back, pumping at the brakes. The front half turned back, and I felt the drag of the trailer as it hit the verge. There was a sickening scrape as the blown tire went off the edge, and I was thrown forward as the drag slowed Dick down. Then the wheel ripped back onto the road, and there was a forward lurch. I pumped the brakes and knew we were now heading for the opposite verge, still going too fast.

I'd rarely been as scared—and never while driving. I hung onto the wheel again, this time pulling right. I was glad at that moment that almost no one drives that road at night, knowing we were slowing down and that if I could hold on for just a little longer, it might be okay. Why in hell hadn't I just stayed in Nata?

We shuddered down the road, scraping the verge twice more before coming to a stop. I got out, shaking, and looked at the vehicle that had slewed across the two lanes, a wheel from each corner touching the fatal edge.

"Good boy, Dick," I said, my voice disappearing into the clear night air. The engine still ran—the sound somehow sacrilegious in such a place, after such an event. I turned the engine off and walked a bit, head down and shaking from adrenalin. I thanked Dick again, feeling grateful for his reluctance to part with the tar, and then heard something in the distance.

A real rig was coming, three or four times Dick's size, and I had the lights off.

I ran back—fast—jumped in, turned everything on, and was sure without checking that Dick's brake lights didn't work and the rig wouldn't see us. I put Dick into first and rumbled him off the road, over the edge, and into the sage just as the rig blasted by, its horn bellowing.

The blast of sound lasted what felt like a long time, then all went quiet again, except a quiet buzz that at first I blamed on stress-induced tinnitus. Then the fine hairs on my ears sent a message to my brain that let me know that I was about to be bitten, and I swatted at the mosquito that had landed. Soon the drone of mosquito buzzing filled the air, and it hurried me out of the cab to figure out how to change Dick's blown wheel without a jack.

There was a shovel mounted behind the cab, and I knew that if I chocked up the axle I could dig under the burst wheel and change it. But there are no rocks in the Madgkadigkadi Pans, and the nearest trees that I could take a branch from were back in Nata. I pondered, swatted, swore, and paced and then heard another jackal bark. There were no donkeys here I could commandeer, I thought, and ride to Maun for help.

However, there were brown hyenas in these parts, a rare animal that I had never seen. I considered playing dead to see if I could attract one—just to have a look at it. This ridiculous thought made me realize that the drinks still had me addled, even if they weren't keeping me awake anymore. Now it was the mosquitoes that ensured I wouldn't fall asleep. I paced around Dick, losing more blood to the most vicious attack any animal had launched on me since the dog when I was seven.

My pacing led me by the back of the cab, where there was a wheel mounted. Then under the trailer I saw another. Two spare tires!

I took one off its mounting, placed it under the rear axle, and dug under the crippled tire, which had been brutally mangled when it dragged over the verge. The vehicle sagged, then held, and soon I had a hole deep enough to remove the tire. I went to the cab, grabbed the wrench, and put it over the nut, knowing straight away that it was way too loose. Dick's nuts at the back were smaller than those at the front. The trailer half had different tires than the Land Rover half had. I looked at the two spares. One was for the front, one for the back. The one for the back, which I needed, was supporting the rear axle. The Madgkadigkadi is an easy place to believe in ancient gods, and right now I knew they were having a grand chuckle at my expense.

I knew that getting the tire off might prove too great a challenge for me, but it was pointless to even try until I had the right spare ready. I had placed what I now thought of as the not-spare under the main arm of the axle, which is not the lowest point. The differential is about three inches lower, and wriggling under the vehicle, banging and scraping my elbows and wrists, I wedged the spare-spare tire under the differential, then dug out the not-spare again, and thought about my wrench issues.

"What would MacGyver do?" I asked myself. But having lived in a tent for too many years without television, I had only heard of the show, so drew little inspiration and wondered what even the most ingenious of action heroes could do with only sand and bad-tasting herbs for resources.

The mosquitoes were now more than just pesky, and I was sure I was getting close to anemic. Perhaps they were getting high on the caffeine in my system and buzzing off to tell all their friends about a great new place to eat, because they were smothering me. They bit my legs, my arms, and my face—even my eyelids were swelling.

Many of the local guides had told me that wild sage is thrown into village fires to ward off the bloodsucking bastards, so I grabbed fistfuls, rubbing it together to release its oils and then dragging the pungent mix over my face and body.

They kept coming, so I grabbed more branches and shoved them down my shirt, into my sleeves, down the front of my shorts, and even under my sandals (though not even the most hungry of mosquitoes had stooped so low as to lick my feet after twelve hours of driving). I heard a rig coming and thought the driver might by some chance have the wrench I needed. My shyness made me stupid, though, and instead of waving him down, I just stood beside Dick and tried to put on a facial expression that suggested a problem tinged with a world-weary forlornness. Maybe the lights canceled out the expression, or maybe I just looked as ridiculous as I was being, but the truck blew past, rocking Dick's front on his springs, his injured half remaining rigid in the sand.

"Not your fault, Dick," I said, knowing that nobody would hear me speaking to a Land Rover, and not caring if they did.

I went back to the wrench problem, exhausted and wishing I was three again so I could just sit, weep, and let an adult deal with it. I tried using my belt buckle, but it broke. I tried packing the wrench I did have with bits of aluminum from the energy drink cans, but it still spun uselessly. I blew dust from my nose, ejecting one or two particularly voracious mosquitoes, and stomped around, angry with the world—but not for long because I knew it was my fault. Dick needed a jack, and I had passed on two opportunities to get one.

"Bugger-shit-piss-wee," I said aloud, something my sister used to say when we were kids, again not caring how ridiculous it sounded. "Bugger-shit-piss-wee," I said again softly. I estimated that I had been working on the problem for about two hours, but it may have been more or less.

Then I gave up.

The mosquitoes could have me. And in the morning some driver would find my desiccated form next to Dick, and my gravestone would read: HERE LIES PETER ALLISON. HE WAS RIDICULOUS. The melodrama lasted only a few moments before a particularly painful bite on the nostril snapped me out of it. I looked at the trailer half. The company wanted to use Dick to transport food to mobile safari operators, so it was airtight at the back and insulated.

I slid the side door open as quickly as I could and clambered in, figuring I would bed down for the night using my shirt as a pillow. I slammed the door shut, sure that in the few seconds it was open not too many mosquitoes could have followed me. But they had, and soon enough I was back outside sinking into despair and madness. The mosquitoes, swarmed, buzzed, dived, and bit; I flailed, cursed, stomped, and bled.

Another truck came by, which would prove to be the last one of the night, and this time I cast shyness aside and stood right beside the road, waving my arms, this time with an unfeigned look of desperation on my features.

The truck blew his horn and blew past, and I realized that the driver would have seen what looked like a very animated sage bush with pasty white hands growing from it. In a superstitious country like Botswana, he'd probably go straight to a witch doctor when he got to Maun and ask if there was a curse on him.

The wind from the truck almost blew me off my feet, but for a few seconds it did clear the air of mosquitoes. Then I heard a buzz, then another, then more, and I had an idea.

I ran. I ran from the mosquitoes, away from Dick, and down the road. Then I stopped, gasping, and enjoyed a brief respite as the mosquitoes sought me out. Then the buzzing came again, and I ran back, putting my hand on Dick's hood as I drew breath. Somewhere a zebra called, and it gave me heart, as animals always do.

I ran away again and again, my sprints getting slower and not as far, and heard the zebra again. I touched the ground, pushed off, ran into the night, and paused, registering that the zebra had just given an alarm call.

Suddenly Dick looked very far away, and I strained my ears to hear over the already swarming insects. The zebras again gave the strange whistle that indicates they have seen danger, but in the best of circumstances I can't get a fix on where sound comes from, and it wasn't the zebra's whereabouts that I needed to know anyway. Lion? Leopard?

Whatever you do, don't run, I thought to myself, and in a moment of fatalism sprinted back to the crippled vehicle, throwing open the side door, but stopping before I went in. It was pitch-black, as clouds had blown in, drowning the stars. Cats could see in this darkness, but all I saw were shapes that could be sage or anything else. I got into the trailer half, sliding the door to a chink and watching through it to see if anything came.

Nothing did, and after immeasurable hours that felt like the sun had fallen away into space never to come again, the darkness weakened. Unseen birds warmed their throats with chirps and cackles, then burst into full song, smothering the sound of insects that had been my only companions all night. The sun cracked the wide-open Madgkadigkadi, one of the most beautiful things I have ever seen, and soon after a small car came down the road and stopped for me.

In Maun, I told Alan where Dick was and was given an adjustable wrench, jack, and a skinny man from the Herero tribe named Gideon to drive me back. We changed the tire with remarkable and anticlimactic ease, and I looked for the tracks of a predator but found none. Damn zebras, I thought, grumpy with fatigue.

Gideon drove off, and I got back into Dick and took him the last hundred or so miles into Maun, where I was put onto a plane and flown into camp because one of the guides was sick. I was ushered straight into my regular Land Rover (which had no doors or windshield—and mercifully no trailer), took an afternoon safari that I mumbled all the way through, and then fell asleep at dinner as a guest was talking to me.

A few months later someone told me that a driver had gotten Dick stuck in a sandy track, and an elephant had taken offense, ramming and piercing the radiator with his tusks. Piet, the cranky Dutch mechanic who looked after our company's vehicles, declared him dead, and he was scrapped for parts.

I didn't care if it was ridiculous, it made me very sad.

Ya-ya and Tsetse

I was driving some "Ya-ya" Germans.

I always knew I had Ya-yas almost as soon as they stepped off the plane, because when I said, "Hello, my name is Peter, pleased to meet you," they would just say, "Ya ya" and thrust luggage into the hand I had offered for shaking.

When I drove back to the camp with Ya-yas and would ask if they had been to Africa before, they would answer, "Ya-ya." Hoping it was only a language barrier that divided us, and not just rudeness, I would do a test.

"What color is the sky?" I would ask.

They would look up, bemused. "Blue," they would answer. And inevitably someone in the back would add, just loud enough for me to hear, "Dummkopf."

"Ya-ya," I would say, knowing I was in for a tough few days.

This particular group of Ya-yas was one of the worst. No matter what I showed them, they would sniff, say "Ya-ya," and look around as if waiting for something more spectacular. We saw cheetahs, we saw leopards, we saw elephants, giraffes, hippos, zebras, hyenas, kudu, baboons, monkeys, and more birds than I could list. At each they would sniff disinterestedly and say, "Ya-ya, but vere are ze lions?"

And that was the problem. My fellow guides and I were having an unprecedented level of difficulty finding the biggest of Africa's cats. The normally rarer cheetahs seemed to be on every termite mound, and the normally shyer leopards were caught crossing almost every open plain. But for a first timer to Africa, and some veterans, nothing matters until they have seen a lion. And the Mombo lions, all eight prides of them, were hiding.

I tried my best to entertain the group with stories of the animals they were seeing. I made jokes, I told funny anecdotes, they looked at me with disdain, I shut up.

On the last day with this group, I believed they would be my first guests ever, after many hundreds of game drives, to leave without seeing lions. I made a plan, which promised high reward, but, like every promise of such a nature, involved high risk. We would go to Boro West.

To the south of Mombo Camp ran a long spine of sand. It was an extension of the Kalahari into the oasis of the Okavango, and if you drove it, you were guaranteed to see little except spiky grass and the occasional ostrich. In the lush wetland that surrounded us, the desert patches held little attraction for the wildlife, so they avoided it.

At the end of the road, though, was Boro West. The most beautiful place I have ever seen, it is only accessible for a few months of the year, when the water levels drop. It is a plain of the most verdant green, dotted with the occasional rain tree spreading its even branches and offering shade. On the lawnlike landscape, thousands of antelope graze, as placid as livestock, content with their abundance. The scene is occasionally punctured by a deep green clump of date palms, and under one of these clumps, if you look hard enough, you can always find the Boro lions.

They are the laziest of a lazy species. With food so close by, and water never more than a thirty-second stroll away, they only bother with a territory of three hundred yards by three hundred yards. They don't even hunt. They just wait under the palms, and eventually an antelope will walk close enough for them to whip out a claw and drag it in.

This was what I would show the Germans, I hoped.

I explained the blandness of the drive and the probable reward at the end.

"Ya-ya," they replied.

I drove faster than I usually would, past the animals that we had already seen many times, feeling I was neglecting the less glamorous but still worthy species like tsessebe, bushbuck, buffalo, and warthog.

"Ah, warzenschwein!" they said at the last. For reasons I will never understand, every German visitor I've ever guided has been excited by the sight of warthogs, and then, more mystifying still, has counted them. "Ein, zwei, drei, vier . . . "

When they were done tabulating, we passed through the territory of Martina's Pride, but she was nowhere to be seen. We crossed the Simbira Channel and drove onto the Middle Road to Boro, and the blandness began.

The wheel whipped in my hands, requiring strength to control as the vehicle forged its way through the deep sand ridges.

We drove on and on, the landscape monotonous, the dust cloying. I felt the hairs on the back of my neck stiffen and knew it was the Ya-yas radiating boredom. There was really nothing to show them, but I want people to love the environment, no matter how dull, so I stopped and swung my legs through the cavity where the door would normally be. Gingerly I put my sandal on the ground, then lifted it and showed the sole to the Germans. It was covered with seeds, each with four vicious spikes that gripped into the rubber. Normally these embed themselves into animals' hooves and help spread the species. I explained this, and told them that in summer the plant, called the devil's thorn, carpets the Kalahari with exquisite yellow flowers.

"Ya-ya," they said and looked away. Show us the bloody lions, was what they really meant, and I wondered if even then I would see them smile.

The Land Rover plowed on and reached the sandiest of points, where little grows except the occasional bedraggled acacia tree. I was about to warn the Germans that this was a likely place for tsetse flies when one bit me. The bite is like acupuncture, but without the remedial benefits. It is a short, shocking pierce that always draws blood and usually a collection of swear words. This fly bit me with a particular viciousness, through the shorts and on a delicate place that no man likes to be bitten.

I did the worst possible thing. Instinctively, I swatted.

Only later did I imagine what it must have looked like to the Germans. They would have seen me turn to say something, my face would have contorted in pain, then I would have punched myself in the delicates. With no door to support me, I fell out of the car, and its reliable diesel engine kept it puttering along in the deep tracks for another thirty yards before it stalled.

In the meantime I lay writhing in self-inflicted, tsetse-assisted agony, each writhe letting more devil's thorns enter my skin. I finally stood, plucked thorns from the side of my scalp and legs, and carefully checked my rear before sitting back in my seat. The Germans had remained sitting straight ahead through my entire performance.

I can proudly say that within a few minutes my risk paid off, and we found the Boro Pride. But nothing made me happier than when I had sat back down and saw why the Germans weren't looking at me.

They were smiling.

A Friend in Hand

As a safari guide I was in constant contact with people. For most of my waking hours, I was with clients and it was my job to be "up," a constant source of information and entertainment. Despite this, it is a strangely lonely profession. The tourists I spent most of my time with were not my friends, and rarely became them. They were in my life for two days, maybe three, and whether I had liked them, or they me, it was too brief to form a bond.

I did draw close to my colleagues, as was inevitable. They were the only people near my age that I encountered, and we all shared a love of wildlife and conservation. But I missed some of my old friends, the ones who had known me since I was a shy schoolboy.

I have known Nick since we were ten. We met when my parents moved again and I started a new school. We caught the same train home together in the afternoon and started talking about the things boys talk about, such as fighter planes, whether a lion or a tiger would win a fight, and whether *Mad* magazine was funnier than *Cracked*. After just more than a year, we started attending the same high school and this time rode the same bus. Our friendship firmed, aided by the proximity of where we lived. From the age of twelve we started a tradition of creeping from our homes to meet at midnight, never to do anything malicious or even devious, just to talk. While any of the Africans that I know would laugh at the idea of my childhood being difficult, it was certainly not a happy one, and it was on these walks that I told Nick of my concern about my father's drinking or that my stepmother was more than a little imbalanced. He rarely offered advice, which was okay because he gave the one thing that I needed—a sympathetic ear.

Our friendship grew strong enough that Nick took the hallowed place and official title of "Best Friend," a position that I had never realized was so good to have filled. We were confidants and brothers, helping each other with things like getting after-school jobs and speaking frankly for the first time about the most fascinating animal of all—woman.

This was a subject on which Nick was clearly the master, and I the bumbling apprentice. We attended a boy's school but caught a public bus that was also a ride for girls who attended many different schools. Watching them get on and off the bus, I would fantasize about speaking to them—just talking—and imagine that I would have things to say that were witty and charming and would make me intensely attractive. The hole in the fantasy was that I had no idea what these words could possibly be, and the very thought of speaking to a girl without a prepared dialogue made my armpits sweat profusely, something undesirable even in a fantasy world.

Nick had no such qualms. He approached girls (for that was what they were, we were only in our early teens) with the same confidence that he approached all life. Nick was the sort of guy who you could throw any object to and he would snatch it effortlessly from the air, and do so with a casual flair. To someone as unathletic as me (I once fractured my collarbone while jogging), this imbued him with almost magical abilities. He was like one of those characters in Greek myths who came about after a god hit the booze and procreated with a mortal.

I used to watch him with a confusing mixture of envy and awe as he casually approached a girl, any girl, and said, "Hi. How are you doing? I like your Walkman. It's cool."

What panache!

There was no way I could emulate him. I was cripplingly shy, and if I had tried such a thing it could only end in disaster. I could imagine the scenario and was sabotaged even in my daydreams. "Hi. How are you doing," I would swallow loudly. "I like your ears. They're cool." A blank look would greet this. "I mean your earplugs. I mean headphones. I'll go away now."

■ ■

Years passed, as they so rudely do, and Nick and I found ourselves separated, often for years at a time. He was as in love with Asia as I was with Africa. I spent two months with him in Indonesia while on the way to settle in South Africa, but it was many years until he was able to visit me. By then I was living in Botswana and had become an experienced guide with a certain degree of respect from my peers.

Despite the subservience of always being nice to people, my confidence had skyrocketed. I had found my place in Africa, and for the first time in my life I knew I was good at something. I looked forward to Nick seeing me in this new environment that I had made my own.

One of the directors of the company was at the airstrip with me when Nick was due to arrive. Despite the positive response I usually received from guests, I'd always had the feeling that this guy didn't like me, which made me nervous around him and more inclined to do things that would exacerbate any idea he might have that I was an idiot. I watched Nick through the grimy window of the Cessna as it taxied toward us. He wetly smooched against the window, and I thought of how much that would impress my boss. When he stepped from the plane, he spread his arms and, exaggerating every word announced to Africa, "I! AM! SO! FUCKING! TIRED!"

My boss raised an eyebrow. This was not the behavior wanted from someone who was staying at the camp for free when everybody else there was paying more than seven hundred dollars a night. I bustled Nick away and got him back to camp, explaining along the way that he might need to temper his language around the sensitive ears of the paying punters.

Through our youth I'd had many reasons to believe that Nick was somehow blessed—among our friends he was the only one whose parents were still together, he had his fantastic coordination, and he possessed charm and confidence. Now I was amazed at how his luck followed him all the way to Botswana, as the very first animal we saw was a cheetah. As I explained to Nick that this was somewhat extraordinary, and that he would be truly considered a favorite of the gods if he was to see it sprint, the cheetah dropped into a crouch and started stalking some impala at the edge of the plain.

She exploded from her standing position but had mistimed her charge, so the impalas had just enough time to make it to the safety of thick bush, where their pursuer's speed was moot. Nick's luck had not run out, though, and as the cheetah turned to settle and recuperate, she flushed an aardwolf from its burrow.

"Holy shit!" I exclaimed, as the hyena-shaped but inoffensive animal ran past us. "This is only the third time I've ever seen one of those!"

"Nice," said Nick. "But I thought we weren't meant to swear."

Nick's plane had come in later than usual, so all the guests were out on a drive when we got in to camp. I gave Nick a quick walk through of Mombo, excited to show it off to someone who knew me from the time when I was just a suburban boy, living behind picket fences and a sturdy tiled roof. As we passed through the office, I heard the guides talking on the radio. From how fast they were speaking and the rapidly changing directions they were giving, it could only mean they were following one thing.

"They've got the dogs," I told Nick, who looked as perplexed as I had wanted him to.

"Is it curable?" he asked.

I didn't respond, just listened to the radio. From the sound of it, the pack, which had seven dogs in it, was heading right for the camp. It was getting close to dusk, and I knew the dogs liked a drink before they settled down for the night.

"Come on," I grabbed Nick. "This is something no tourist gets to do."

He was still jet-lagged and weary enough to follow without questioning, and as I took him out to the back of the camp and the ever-productive waterhole that was formed by washing our Land Rovers, I told him about the dogs.

"They're the most endangered and least known of Africa's large carnivores." I was speaking like a guide to my oldest friend, but I was too excited to drop into colloquialisms. "Most places they've been shot out or killed by diseases that they catch from domestic dogs, but we see a fair amount of them here, and following them when they hunt is the most fun you can have in a Land Rover without getting someone pregnant." That was more like how we usually spoke.

I could hear the vehicles that were following now and knew they would move away before the dogs reached the unsightly back half of the camp where the waterhole was. This left us free to do what I wanted without being observed by tourists.

"Lie down," I told Nick, and I reposed myself next to his obediently sprawled form. In the dwindling light the silhouette of the dogs appeared, coming at a trot right for us. "Nothing is as successful as these guys at hunting. They're like wolves. They just run and run and run, until their prey is exhausted. Then they disembowel it, which is messy looking, but more efficient than strangling like the cats do." I paused, watching as the dogs slowed to walk, sniffing as they approached us. "When the dogs hunt, they kill." I was loving this, and looked at Nick's face to see if he was having as much fun. He didn't appear to be at all enjoying the sight of the seven dogs that were now directly opposite us, sniffing and making the occasional low growl. "Of course," I whispered, "there's no record of them attacking people, so this is relatively safe."

The dogs started drinking, having determined that we were not a threat. I felt Nick relax beside me. I was glad that he had started enjoying the experience, but also took a secret thrill from having seen him out of his element in a place where I was so comfortable.

I had guests arrive the next morning so was busy working most of the time that Nick stayed, but he still managed to get out on a number of drives with me, and his luck continued. He saw abundant lions, had fantastic leopard sightings, drove alongside the dogs as they hunted, and got up close to elephants. On his final morning one of the other guides found a cheetah that was well-known to all of us. She had three cubs that were almost fully grown, and all of them were incredibly relaxed around the vehicles.

It was reported that the cheetahs weren't doing much, so I took my time getting there, spending some time with reliably amusing baboons and always impressive giraffes. All the other guides had left when I arrived where they had been watching the cheetah. And despite their assertions that she was lying flat with the cubs and wasn't going anywhere, I couldn't see her. There were tracks for all four cheetahs walking farther into the open plain, but I couldn't see them anywhere out there either. I followed the tracks and saw that the cheetahs had made an abrupt turnabout and headed into the treeline. I was scanning these with my binoculars when I heard a telltale snort.

"Watch this!" I shouted, as a herd of impala thundered out of the bush, into the plain. I knew the antelopes had made a mistake. They should have stayed in the trees, where their leaping would have kept them safe from the cheetahs' straight-line pace. Instead they were now running in the open, following a line that would take them a few yards in front of the hood of our Land Rover. The cheetahs burst out behind them and were easily overtaking them. The impalas started to jink and sidestep, hoping the pursuers would overshoot the mark, but they had come too far into the open. The mother cheetah tapped the ankle of an impala, and as it rolled, she gripped its throat with her teeth.

The dust settled, and the excited cubs gave out little twitters as they tried to help, making attempts to strangle the already dead impala's leg, ear, and hoof. The mother allowed their experiments as she recovered her breath, panting deeply to get oxygen into her system and reduce her lactic acid buildup. After a few short moments, she stood up and hauled the carcass under the nearest bush, a low and prickly acacia. The entire action had taken only a few minutes, throughout which I had said nothing.

"That was spectacular!" said one of my guests. But the rest said nothing, just sat looking shocked. While many people came to Africa in the hope of seeing exactly this sort of thing, others found a kill distressing, and I waited nervously for the others to digest what they had seen.

"Wow," Nick said quietly. Then he added more emphatically, "Fucking WOW!"

The people in the car looked at him like he was mad, then caught his infectious excitement. I watched it spread from one person to the next. Then they were all talking at once.

"Did you see how fast . . . "

"And then it stepped like this . . . "

"Fast, man, that was faster than a car!"

"Poor thing," said another, dampening the mood.

"Yes, but as this young gentleman said, fucking WOW!" replied an older man who up to that point had been very staid and conservative. Then they were all talking at once again, and laughing, and I knew that it would be the highlight of their trip. I gave

Nick a wink, and he grinned wildly back at me.

After the drive, I grabbed Nick and said, "We're skipping brunch."

"Why?" he asked, quite reasonably, as the omelets were very good.

"We're going to do another thing that no tourist gets to do."

We drove back out to the cheetahs, who were still feeding on the impala. Periodically the mother would sit up and scan the surrounds, wary of hyenas, lions, or a leopard, any of which would steal the meat from her.

"Okay, this is what we're going to do," I instructed. "We'll get out on the opposite side of the Rover and crawl under it until we're about ten yards from them. I don't want to freak them out by going up to them together, so we'll take turns crawling closer. You've got your camera, right?"

The look Nick was giving me was the sort you give to someone who is dribbling as they speak. "What?" I asked him, wiping at my face.

"You are kidding, aren't you?"

"No, I'm serious. It's safe, trust me. We've spent months getting them used to us." From his look, I must have still been dribbling. "This is one of the few times someone will offer you a once-in-a-lifetime opportunity that really is once in a lifetime. I don't know of any wild cats, anywhere else in the world, that you could do this with." He still looked uncertain. "Trust me," I repeated, and got out of the car and started a gentle slither toward the feeding cheetahs. They ignored me, until I was almost on top of them, when one of the youngsters jumped up and hissed at me, stepping closer and snarling again, this time in my face. I knew there were no confirmed records of a cheetah attacking a person in the wild, but it is still terrifying having a big cat show you its teeth at close range, no matter how cool I was acting in front of Nick. The cheetah backed off and playfully cuffed his sister, then kept eating. The mother cheetah sat up, looked around, and in a way that I always found fascinating, looked everywhere but at me, as if she was pretending that I wasn't there or found me so uninteresting that she couldn't bear to look at me.

"You getting photos?" I asked.

"How do you work this radio, so I can call for help when they attack you?" was Nick's reply. I guessed the young male cheetah's approach had looked worse than it was.

"It's fine—he was just playing."

Nick took some photos of me, then I gently coerced him from the vehicle. He was shivering, even though it was a mild morning. "It's okay, they won't hurt you. Even if they come close, it's just play." He gave me the look again, and this time I checked my face. No dribble. He crept closer, then whispered over his shoulder, "You know that I just saw these things rip the throat out of an animal?"

I didn't point out that it wasn't actually that dramatic, that the skin on the impala's neck wasn't even broken. I just nodded to him and gave gentle waves, fanning him forward.

He reached a point and stopped. His body was taut, and something about him seemed entirely unfamiliar. Once or twice in the years we had known each other, I had seen Nick out of his element, but it was only a flicker before he used a chameleon-like ability to adapt to his surrounds and the people within it. But now he was afraid, something I had never seen. "Stop," I said. "I'll get some shots of you there." His posture showed relief, then with visible reluctance he turned his back to the cheetahs and looked at the camera. His face was grim. "Try and smile," I said. "Your mother will prefer it."

"My mother always thought you were a bad influence. Showing her photos of this would only confirm it."

"Right," I said, and clicked the shutter, capturing Nick with the spotted cats behind him and an expression on his face suggestive of constipation.

On the drive back, after a bit of silence, I said, "You know, I wasn't a bad influence. I was only ever there when you got in trouble because I was trying to talk you out of something. You should tell your mother that."

"Before or after I tell her that you tried to feed me to some cheetahs?"

We drove on, and I reflected on the pleasure that I had felt from seeing Nick in a situation where he wasn't totally confident. I wondered if there was something wrong with me for enjoying so much seeing him look less like a god and more like a mortal. Then I realized there was nothing wrong with how I had felt. Seeing Nick vulnerable hadn't made me respect him any less, or change the value of our friendship.

In fact, I liked him even more.

Bad Actors

When you work in any form of tourism, you come to understand how the stereotypes of certain countries form and can dread encounters with people based solely on their nationality. As a safari guide, however, you spend more time with individual clients than you would working in a hotel, so you get to see beyond the arrogance of the French, the volume of the Americans, the snobby reservedness of the English, the drunkenness of the Australians, and the utter lack of humor of the Germans. It teaches you not to judge someone just because of where they are from, and to stop refusing to guide New Yorkers. Not all people are defined by the place they are from. On occasion, though, an individual appears who seems determined not to break the mold in which their nationality is cast, but to reinforce it.

Such a man was Spiirubaagu, as he came to be known on his brief safari in Northern Botswana. He epitomized the image of the Japanese tourist who always has a camera in his hand and will take a photograph of anything. I pitied whomever would be forced to endure his slide shows as he snapped away at the tent he stayed in, the bed in his tent, the wardrobe in his tent, the zipper on his tent, the luggage in his tent. These were just the shots taken while inside, and he took painstaking care in setting up each shot, ensuring his focus and subject were just right.

It was actually rare for us to have Japanese tourists at our camp, mainly because the Japanese usually travel in large groups and want their own food, and we only had twenty beds and cooked whatever we could get flown in from the nearest town. Yet once or twice a year, a group of intrepid Japanese would arrive. And as I spoke a little of the language, it was inevitable that I would be allocated to guide them.

The first sign that something was wrong was the way the plane landed. The pilots in the Okavango are good—really good. They land and take off more times in a day than almost any other commercial pilots in the world, and they do it on dirt strips with unusual crosswinds, sporadic dust storms, and the more than occasional animal that wanders onto the field. So it struck me as odd the way the twin-engine whumped down, hitting hard onto the strip and not bouncing back up like a light aircraft should. It taxied over, and the pilot shook his head at me through his window.

Then came the second sign of problems brewing. First out of the plane were two twenty-something girls who had obviously thought long and hard about the suggested khaki-colored clothes for safari and had rejected the prospect. They were arrayed in a clash of canary yellow and a shade of pink so lurid it could make Barbie puke. Most animals are color-blind, so it wasn't really a problem, but I was always nervous about people who were defiant in a place where the wrong behavior could get you eaten.

As the seventh person exited the aircraft and started hauling out his gear, my foreboding increased. Any travel agent stresses to a client that they will be traveling in very small bits of motorized tin, and their luggage weight should reflect that. In fact, it is set at a strict twenty-five pounds. But looking at the camera bags and tripods being wrestled from the cargo area, I could tell that this guy had gone well over that. There was only one way he could have achieved this, and it would have involved a feigned or real misunderstanding of English when the pilot protested.

■ ■

"We almost died." It was the pilot, his New Zealand accent being pushed through clenched teeth. "We were overweight, because every time I tried to take a bag out, he just said 'Hai' and shoved it back in. Then, in midflight, he started taking photos, which was no problem, but when I pointed out some hippos, he leaned over the top of me and shoved me into the controls." He gave a hiss to show how stupid this was. "Not one of them screamed when we went into a dive. What sort of people are they?"

He wasn't looking for an answer, so I didn't give him one. We both knew anyway. These sort of people could be from any country. They thought that Africa was a theme ride and didn't take its dangers seriously. They were a hazard to themselves and to anyone who had to keep them out of harm's way—like me.

I looked at the vehicle, which the group had swarmed on to take their seats. It now bristled with tripods and lenses. They looked back at me, smiling.

"Ikimashoo ka?" I asked. "Shall we go?"

There was a flurry as it dawned on them that I had spoken in their language, which rose to a hubbub before settling down to polite introductions.

"And you must be Spielberg," I said to the one with all the

camera gear, including an expensive-looking video rig. Su-pee-ra-bar-gu is how it is pronounced in Japanese, and they all laughed. It's the sort of inoffensive joke you are always making when people are paying for you to be nice to them. Spiirubaagu just smiled, and without preamble said, "I would like to film a lion killing something."

I could tell by the way he said it that he considered himself somewhat magnanimous to not be specific about the prey. I wanted to explain that when he watched a documentary, the half hour of footage he saw probably took more than a year to film, that the makers of it spent every waking hour and more in the bush, enduring months of tedium for the one gory moment of triumph—but unfortunately my Japanese isn't that good.

"We'll see," I said instead, and we started making our way to the camp. Along the rough track that led back to camp, we saw our first animals, and after their reaction I was forced to explain the fundamental thing that guides hate most to have to explain.

"How's your group?" my friend Lloyd, the manager, asked once we were in the camp.

"I had to tell them the basics," I said.

"No!"

"True."

"In English or Japanese?"

"Bit of both. Most of it in Japanese, the swear words in English."

Lloyd pondered this. "Are you sure they understood?"

"I think so, yeah, I'm pretty sure."

"Because one of them is on the deck throwing bread to a warthog."

"Shit," I said, and went off to repeat the speech I had already made in the vehicle after the group had leapt from the vehicle on masse. The exodus occurred because we had seen some impala, which had scattered in panic at the marauders. These were not zoo animals, I explained. They were wild. We didn't feed them, stroke them, or stand next to them for photographs. In fact all we did was watch them live and die. I was, in fact, thankful for the little incident and that the first thing we had seen had been an antelope herd. If we'd encountered an elephant, it might have made my point for me, but with a lot less delicacy. This happy fantasy sustained me while I reiterated my point to the young lady who was lobbing crusts at the bemused but not ungrateful pig.

The game drives proceeded relatively well during their stay, though Spiirubaagu insisted on giving stage directions to every animal we saw and grew increasingly frustrated at their inability to understand him. One species had him particularly vexed.

For some reason that no behaviorist has ever explained, zebras are the most notorious bum flashers. You can guarantee every time you are ready to take their photo that they will turn and show off their striped derriere. After perhaps the thirtieth such time that Spiirubaagu had faced such an indignity, he shouted at the zebra to stand still.

"These animals only speak Setswana," I said facetiously. "Ask the staff to teach you some." Later that evening I saw him in earnest conversation with Mollen, our barman, who spoke limited English and to the best of my knowledge spoke not a word of Japanese.

"Yes!" I would hear the ever-cheerful Mollen say periodically. "This is Botswana!"

Clearly they had a communication breakdown, because while I listened for and looked forward to hearing Japanese-accented Setswana commands given to the animals, I never heard one. Spiirubaagu did use some of the rare Japanese expletives, though. (It is a language almost devoid of swear words, and it is only with great creativity that you can insult as foully as is possible in English.) His tirade was directed at a giraffe, one of the few animals that had actually appeared to follow his directions. Briefly anyway.

The giraffe had been feeding on a tall acacia tree, his head buried deep in the thorny branches, rendering him unphotographable. When he was done, it would seem most likely that he would head deeper into the thicket of trees to feed some more, rather than the more aesthetically pleasing option of crossing the open plain behind him.

"Come out," Spiirubaagu commanded.

Miraculously, the giraffe did. It made its stately way for two of its long swinging paces, then stopped to face us. A million-dollar-a-day supermodel couldn't have posed more splendidly.

Then again, the supermodel probably wouldn't start to openly urinate either, which is what the giraffe did. The stream came thick and gooey, and I explained to the group that giraffes are at their most vulnerable to lions when they lean down to drink, so they do everything they can to conserve water—including a biological process that leaves their piss thick and honeylike.

The incensed Spiirubaagu was shouting at the giraffe (another thing I had repeatedly asked the group not to do was call out to the animals, but this was too amusing for me to stop him), "Stop pissing! Stupid animal! Can't you see I'm trying to take your photo!"

Once again, the giraffe appeared to listen. After a last few stringy gloops, it stood magnificently posed for just a moment, with the glorious green backdrop of the Okavango framing it. Then too quickly for Spiirubaagu to gather his wits and focus, the giraffe promptly stepped back into the acacias and walked away.

■ ■

On our last drive together, we had set out for a particularly beautiful part of the Okavango, where huge herds of antelope could be found on a permanently green plain. I was always open to disruption to my plans, because if we didn't reach a destination it could only mean that we had found something better to look at.

So it was with no disappointment that I saw fresh lion tracks on the dirt road we were using. With no thought as to how hypocritical it might look, I stepped out of the vehicle to take a better look. (Guides do this all the time: insist it is way too dangerous for anyone else to get out of the car, or even stand up in it, then stroll around themselves as if their khaki uniform makes them invulnerable.) The tracks were really fresh.

"Very new, only a few minutes old," I told the group, following the tracks a little farther along the soft dust of the road. "It's an adult female. No, two adult females." I knew these lions. We were in the territory of Martina's Pride, a small group of only two adults (in which one of the females was unusually large and even more bizarrely had a scraggly mane). I suspected that the nonhairy female had given birth to cubs recently, so I was excited that we might see them.

To make sure that the lions hadn't just crossed the road and moved into the thick bush on my left, I walked a little farther, not thinking of how much I was isolating myself from the vehicle. I was hoping that the lions would be somewhere on the plains to my right, where it would be easier to spot them.

"Hey!" I shouted back to the eager faces who were peering over the back of the open-topped Land Rover. "There're tracks for little cubs here!" I took a few more steps.

"It looks like the cubs went this way," I pointed into the bush. "And the adults went this way," I said, aiming my other arm out toward a complex of termite mounds. Then, still in the cruciform position, I spoke, this time only to myself.

"Stupid. Stupid. Stupid. Stupid," and at the fourth stupid, they came at me.

■ ■

When you are training to be a guide, you learn that the African bush is a much safer place than you might imagine. Once you have learned a few rules, you are less likely to get injured than a person in the city who faces traffic every day. Dealing with the dangerous animals becomes something as habitual as looking both ways when you cross a road.

What you also learn is that there are things you can do in the bush that are like crossing a busy road with your eyes shut and ears blocked. The first thing they teach you as a guide is that you never get between a lion and her cubs. It's the second thing they teach you as well, just to reinforce it, and usually they reiterate it a third time for good measure.

I'd just forgotten to look both ways, and Martina and her sister, who I had seen ripping other animals to pieces on a number of occasions, were coming at me.

I felt naked and cold, despite the desert sun. I let the training that I had not forgotten take over. My arms were already raised, which had the advantage of making me look bigger. I turned to the lions, front on, showing that I had forward-facing eyes, like them and all other predators. This is meant to make them hesitate. I tried to roar, but as always happened to me in these circumstances what came out was more of a pathetic whimper.

They weren't coming in a straight line at me, but were bouncing stiff-legged from side to side, getting incrementally closer. This, the books tell you, is an almost sure sign of a mock charge, and the lions will probably stop before they get to you and will then back off.

The knowledge that the lions weren't sure yet that they were going to kill me was little comfort, and I was barely relieved when they stopped about twenty feet from me. They backed slowly away, the ridge of fur along their spine erect, their faces twisted into snarls, and low growls emanating and filling the air, seeming to come from every direction at once.

I took a step back.

They came again, bouncing once more from side to side, stopping closer to me than the time before. Again, the roar I gave was less than threatening. They backed away, bellies low to the ground, their focus as unwaveringly on me as mine was on them. When they stopped, tails twitching, I took a step back again. They charged.

Three times they came at me, their bouncing run impossible to track—yellow fur and a fury of teeth—as they homed in.

The fourth time they backed off, I stepped back again, getting another pace closer to the safety of the vehicle. This time when they came, they came straight.

This is it, I thought, and gave maybe the only roar that I have ever managed that had some menace in it. They didn't slow, and it took only a second before they were at me.

They ran straight past, close enough for me to reach out a hand and touch them, before I could even register that they weren't going to hit me. All that was left was a hole in the bush they had plunged through and their pungent odor as they had headed for the cubs they had been protecting.

I wanted to sit down, but I did the right thing and continued slowly, shakily, backing away. At the vehicle I finally turned. Somehow all seven of the Japanese had squeezed onto the seat at the back of the vehicle (which is designed for three) to lean over and watch. Spiirubaagu had his video camera hanging loosely in his hand, lens cap on, a look of displeasure on his face.

As I staggered into my seat, wanting to cry, wanting to puke, wanting to laugh and scream, he spoke.

"I'm sorry, but I wasn't able to get that the first time. Would you mind doing it again?"

Bale and the Snake

Of all the workers building Duba Camp, Bale was the only one causing any trouble. His name was pronounced in two separate syllables, and many times throughout the day you could hear one of the foremen shout, "Ba-le! What are you doing!?"

"Nothing," Bale would reply, quite honestly.

If it was pointed out that this was a problem, as he wasn't being paid to do nothing, he would shrug, smile, and say, "Okay." As if to say, that's your problem, not mine—which left the foremen with a quandary. There were few jobs they trusted Bale to do that he wouldn't stuff up. In the crew of workers, there were skilled wood-carvers making decorations, skilled carpenters building decks, skilled laborers putting up the huge tents for the guests to sleep in, and Bale, who was skilled only at avoiding work.

Despite this, I liked him. He laughed easily and honestly and was brazen in asking for money when he already owed me a fortune, an unusual bravery that for reasons unknown I found admirable. Another trick of his was to ask me for cigarettes every day, even though I don't smoke.

"I don't smoke, Bale," I would say, beginning the ritual.

"Then buy me a cigarette," he would smile.

"They're bad for you. Go and do some work."

"Work. Maybe it is bad for me too." And he would saunter off, seeking a shady tree where he might go undisturbed for hours. Since I was not involved directly in the construction, it was harder for me to dislike him than it was for the builders.

I was taking over as manager of the camp when it opened, and by the predictions of the builders the camp would not be ready. We were also low on stock of things the camp would need to function, such as cooking pots and beds. Gavin and Attie, the two builders, were commandeering every flight and filling it with building material, and I was starting to stress that not only would the first guests have no rooms to sleep in, but no food to eat either. I walked to the dry-goods storeroom to check the stocks of flour, and I trod on a snake.

"Buggershitpisswee!" I shouted as I jumped back and dropped to a boxing stance. I don't know boxing, and it wouldn't work against snakes, but it always makes me feel better after a fright to look like I'm ready for anything.

My martial ineptitude was not a factor in this instance, though. The snake was dead. It was not my boot that had caused it either, but something bigger and heavier. By the look of the mangled body, it had been smashed, repeatedly and cruelly. In the corner of the storeroom was a brick, and I suspected it to be the murder weapon.

"Damn, bro, that's cruel," said a voice behind me, startlingly close. I spun and went into my boxing pose again. This was just as ineffective against the man who stood in front of me as it would be with the snake, because he was one of those characters who had done a bit of everything in his life, including a stint as a Thai boxer. His name was Anthony, and he was in camp helping with the building.

I came out of my squat and dropped my hands, which he had politely not commented on, and said, "Yeah, this is the third one I've found. I'm calling a staff meeting."

Anthony looked at the snake and said, "Not even poisonous." I knew, as did he, that that didn't matter to the staff. Most Africans distrust and are fearful of every snake, no matter its size or toxicity.

■ ■

I got on well with the staff at Duba, because I only lose my temper once a year and am able to treat most things as a joke. The only thing that ever gets me riled is cruelty. It makes my jaw clench and a blood red veil drop over my eyes. But the worst thing is that the filter between my brain and mouth disappears, and I say things that cannot be taken back.

The staff watched me quietly at the meeting. They could tell I was angry by the pulsing vein in my forehead and the audible grinding of my teeth.

"Who's killing snakes?!" I demanded shrilly. No answer. "Come on! Who killed the snake in the storeroom?" Their blank stares infuriated me. I scanned the assembled group for a guilty look, but they remained impassive. Only Bale showed any emotion. He was grinning, as he did whenever he wasn't snoring.

Anthony saw I was about to lose it and say something stupid, so he stepped in. "Guys, if any of you see a snake, don't kill it. Come and get me. I'll catch it and drive it out into the bush for four miles. No snake has a territory bigger than that, so it won't be able to find its way back."

The staff started nodding, but I was still angry. "Yeah, and if I catch anyone killing a snake, or any animal, I'll drive them four miles into the bush and see if they make it back." I was given the contemptuous stares I deserved, and the staff wandered off.

■ ■

Two weeks later, one staff member took Anthony up on his offer and we drove a furious Egyptian cobra four miles into the bush and dumped it out of the burlap sack we had carried it in. The staff members were happy to be taken seriously, and I found no more dead snakes.

I wouldn't have had time to do anything about them anyway. Unseasonable rain had pushed the building schedule back, and guests were about to start flying in. Tents were only half built, the main area leaked, and the furthermost tents still didn't have a path to them. Everyone in camp was busy in a frenzy of activity. The laundry ladies who normally washed and ironed the clothes of the tourists were swinging hammers, the kitchen staff were cutting dead trees into logs to mark out the pathways, the guides were stocking the bar, I was digging holes, and Bale was walking between each group, offering commentary but no assistance.

Gavin and Attie had threatened to fire him on numerous occasions, but they knew Botswana's labor laws don't allow dismissal due to laziness. Unless he took too many sick days or was caught stealing, we were stuck with him. On the day the first guests were flying in, a spurt of energy pushed us all to finish the last few tents, patch the leaks, and have ice-cold drinks in time for their arrival. Bale had been given the incomparably simple job of laying straight poles on each side of the pathways. Even this seemed too much for him, because I found him strolling toward me, tunelessly whistling, with a big smile.

"I can't work!" he told me proudly.

"Yes, Bale, I know that, but specifically, this time, why?" My patience was thin, and for once I wasn't amused by his boldness.

"There's a big nyooka beside the path." Nyooka is the Setswana word for snake. "I can't work," he added again.

"What sort of nyooka, Bale?" I imagined a mamba, cobra, or possibly a python.

"A big one!"

It wasn't as specific as I would have liked.

I followed him down the unbordered and dusty path, and under an acacia bush was a python. It had a broad head and dark markings, like an older python does, but I could see its tail and overall it didn't look that big. I'd sworn off picking up snakes, because I had learned the hard way that I wasn't very good at it. But the temperature was cool, I imagined the snake would be sluggish, and it wasn't that big a python.

I grabbed it behind the head with my left hand and lunged for the tail with my right, grabbing it above the place any feces would come from if it ejected some (another lesson I had learned the hard way). I stood upright and knew my mistake. The python had been sitting in a hole, and while I had both ends, there was a lot more to its middle than I had foreseen.

The snake's mouth opened, showing the curved and jagged daggers of its teeth.

"Now you'll die," said Bale, without a hint of remorse. "It's poison."

I didn't answer. I just wondered how I was going to put it down without getting bitten. It was more than ten feet long and apparently quite unhappy with me. It writhed in my hands, and it took all of my recently acquired builder's muscle to contain it. It made a loop of its body, which slid onto my right hand, covering its tail. It defecated, and the stink was overwhelming. There is something about a six-month digestive process that really gets a pong going. It threw another coil, and my arm started to get weighed down.

"Bale! Come and hold its head so I can unwind it."

"Uh-uh. It's poison," he said, squatting so he was more comfortable while he watched the show.

"Bale, it's a python. It's not poisonous. They kill by strangling." A process the python was starting on my arm. My fingers were turning red, but they held their grip, slippery as it was with slick snake shit.

"Uh-uh," Bale said again. "Even if you touch them, they're poison." I didn't have time to correct his English, let alone thousands of years of cultural beliefs, as my fingers were now purple. The python was drawing my two arms together so he could loop himself right over me, and I was losing the strength to fight him.

"Go get Anthony. Tell him I need help."

"Okay," Bale said, and began a slow amble along the path, whistling as he went.

"Bale!" He turned, and I thrust the snake toward him as if to throw it. "Run!"

He broke into a marathoner's shuffle and disappeared around a bush.

I spent all of my energy keeping my two arms apart. I knew if the python linked them or got any more coils around, I would be severely bitten. Rationally I knew that it wouldn't eat me, but the constant hissing and lunging made it seem as if it might try. A Cessna flew over low and waggled its wings, getting ready to land. I wondered if any of the incoming tourists had seen the strange sight on the ground and what they would think if they had. The snake hissed at the plane and redoubled its efforts to cut off the blood flow to my arm.

The fingers of my right hand had taken on an ominous silver grey sheen and were losing their grip on the tail. I dropped to one knee, putting some of the python's weight on the ground. It immediately gripped the earth with its scales and drew me closer to it. I tried to stand again, but I did not have the energy. I was in for one hell of a biting, I was sure. A python's teeth lacerate and leave wounds prone to infection, and I would not have any energy to defend myself.

My strength failed.

Bugger, I thought, and let go of the tail.

A hand shot forward and grabbed it. It was Anthony's. I hadn't seen him coming.

"Good timing," I said, grateful for his appearance.

"I would have been here sooner," Anthony replied. "But Bale told me the wrong place."

"Right," I panted, and with a last bit of strength I helped Anthony throw the struggling snake into a waterhole, where it wouldn't get hurt or be able to hurt us. It slithered out the opposite side and into the bush.

I could hear a Land Rover approaching the camp and knew it was filled with expectant tourists hoping to see magnificent wildlife and hear tales of derring-do.

"I better go and meet the guests," I said, wanting some time to recover but knowing I had none.

"You might want to wash your hands before you shake any of the guests' with them," Anthony said. "They stink of snake shit."

"Yeah, right," I said. Then I had an idea. "But first I'm going to go and shake Bale's."

Encounters with Salvador

There is a specific madness that infects people who live in the bush. They ignore the rational fear that stops an ordinary individual from approaching dangerous animals. This fear diminishes when you live with these animals every day, and you start pushing the boundaries of safe behavior to the breaking point. The very people who expressly forbid tourists from taking the slightest of risks, and get foamy at the mouth with anger when they do, are the same individuals you will find slithering up to large cats on their bellies or holding some of the world's most dangerous snakes in their mouths as a party trick. It is inevitable that this leads to the occasional tragedy, and news is reported of the expert who wasn't quite careful enough. The bush community shake their collective heads, say "Idiot," and then see if they can pluck a hair from an elephant's tail.

Personally, I am not one to take chances with lions, and I avoid buffalo when I can. Crocodiles terrify me, so I never play games with them. And after a few bites, I gave up on handling snakes. I do push the boundaries with my two favorite animals: cheetahs, which aren't known to be dangerous, and elephants, which are.

I like to read an elephant's mood, using body language as a guide, then see how close I can get. The best way to do this is to let them approach me, so I try to figure out which way they are likely to head and place myself in a concealed position where they're about to start feeding. There is no sensation like being within touching distance of the largest land animal in the world, even from the relative safety of a vehicle. My breathing becomes wispy, every nerve is hypersensitive, and my heart races shallowly, as if it knows it must be quiet. Some elephants are never in the mood to tolerate proximity, and it's necessary to keep a distance of many tens of yards or you can end up with considerable damage to your vehicle, your body, and your tourists—and most likely your employer will be upset about at least two.

One elephant, though, is the most tolerant I have ever met, and as she is the leader of a herd, the whole family follows her example. The best experiences I have ever had with elephants have been encounters with Salvador and her herd.

Every year at some point, Salvador's herd arrives at Mombo. It might be during the summer rains, or it might be in the winter when the flood was pushing in. She wasn't living to any schedule, just moving with the food and appearing when it was best for her family to do so. Until I saw her, I had not been paying much attention to the identities of the elephants I saw at Mombo. The bulls that we saw, either by themselves or in small bachelor groups, were usually relaxed with the vehicles and allowed us to get very close. We always treated the herds of females with a little more trepidation, as any species that misinterprets your actions as a threat to its young is dangerous. And this species weighs thousands of pounds and can outrun an Olympic sprinter.

This herd was different. Driving toward them, it was obvious that they were unperturbed by vehicles. They were aware of my presence and that of the Land Rover that I sat in with my guests. Watching closely I could see their eyes turn toward us, then back to their food without hesitation. Occasionally one of the younger males would trot toward the vehicle, ears flared and trunk held high, challenging me to a fight. But this is typical of all little boys, and they try the same bullying tactics on buffalo, giraffes, and even the occasional palm tree. The rest of the family would walk casually around the car, even brushing against it, rocking it on its springs as they did. On these occasions I rarely had to remind my guests that they should stay still and quiet.

With any herd I like to see if I can figure out who the matriarch is, and being so close to this group it was easy. Generally the old female in charge is in the lead when a herd crosses open ground, but disrespectful youngsters sometimes usurp the front position. My method for discerning the leader involved listening. Elephants communicate with one another in a complex language, most of which is at a frequency too deep for a human to hear. One phrase that is audible is a base rumble that sounds like the belly of a hungry giant. This verbal quake means "Let's go." When a group of ellies are feeding, you often hear the younger herd members saying this, obviously bored. "Come on, Mom, Auntie, can we go? Come on, let's go!" The herd ignores the teens, but the moment the matriarch rumbles, the entire group moves at once, forming a line with the youngest at the back.

I identified the leader of this group as a female that I guessed to be somewhere in her forties. She was easy to note, as her tusks grew not forward but extravagantly outward and then up, curling around to each side like Salvador Dali's moustache. I named her Salvador at first sight, irrespective of her gender.

The sweeping teeth that had given her her name protruded wider than her shoulders, but they offered no impediment to her except once when I saw the whole herd pass through two closely growing palm trees that she had to step around. Otherwise she used them to dig up roots, peel bark from trees, and lazily rest her trunk upon, just as other elephants do.

One August morning an unseasonable mist had risen from the diminishing floodwaters and obscured Salvador's herd as I watched her feeding in the trees. I knew when the mist lifted, the light would be perfect for photography and every blade of grass would glisten with dew, sparking little rainbows in the lens. It was an opportunity too good to miss, so after brunch I grabbed two other staff members and my camera and raced back to where I had seen the remarkably relaxed herd.

I was an enthusiastic if untalented photographer and had recently seen some photos that I wished to mimic. They were of an elephant, taken with an expensive and long lens from a low angle, which created the effect of looking up, almost from the elephant's feet. Since I lacked artistic vision, money, and a big lens, I had to use the resources available to me and figure out a way to get extremely close to Salvador while she was so busy doing something that she wouldn't think to tread on me. As the family left the copse they had been stripping for leaves and winter fruits, I saw my opportunity.

"Guys, if we drive into that channel, the herd will be right in front of us when they drink." I already had the engine started.

"Are you sure you want to risk drowning another car?"

Hayden asked. I had no idea how deep the channel was and was under threat of dismissal if another vehicle met a watery end while I was driving it.

I didn't want to risk it, so I came up with another, considerably worse plan that the others wanted nothing to do with.

The channel that I believed the elephants were coming to drink from was not a particularly wide one. It ran deep for only about 6 feet across, but spilled into the floodplain over a width of about 120 yards. This area was dotted with flowers of pink, white, and yellow and dappled with green shoots of aquatic grasses. The deeper water was a dark and menacing blue, and I planned on not getting close enough to it to let a crocodile grab me and pull me into its depths.

As Ella and Hayden sat sensibly in the Land Rover, I stripped down to shorts and waded into the water. It was considerably chillier than I had imagined. Around the ankles it was merely unpleasant, but as I slipped into the occasional divot made by crossing animals, it would splash higher. As it hit my crotch, I gave out a long gasping word "ohmysweetlittlechilliesthatiscold!"

The herd, which had been confidently approaching the channel up until now, heard my exhalation. Some of the leading members paused, raising their trunks to sniff the air. One by one behind them, the younger elephants copied their elders, until the babies at the back also wavered their uncoordinated noses in the air. I sank low into the water, pushing myself firmly into the mud beneath it, holding only my camera above the surface. Salvador strode boldly forward, her ears flared. An elephant's eyesight is not the best, but she would have made out the vehicle on the bank opposite her. And if she had looked closer, she would have made out the unusual sight of a human trying to burrow into mud not far from her feet.

I pulled my head from the mud just in time to see Salvador's posture relax and her trunk droop onto one of her wayward tusks. She hadn't seen me. She walked forward again, and as her feet hit the water she started gripping flowers with her trunk, dragging their tendrils into her mouth and chomping contentedly.

She reached the deeper water at a point opposite me on the channel, and I started shivering with a mixture of cold and excitement. I'd been close to elephants on foot before and always marveled at how significantly more gigantic they appeared when away from the safety of a vehicle. Now, with Salvador and her sweeping tusks looming over my prone form, fear won over my enthusiasm. I started to think that I should have listened to Hayden and Ella.

Salvador started to drink—great slurps with her trunk first, then a slosh as she cocked her head back and released a gushing torrent into her mouth. The occasional splash landed on me, and in a moment of scientific inquiry, I wondered how much bacteria might be up an elephant's nose.

I took some photos with my quaking hands, mainly close-ups of Salvador's broad and flawed face as she drank but also wider shots of the whole herd as they fanned out on either side of her and gurgled at the channel.

Although I was close enough to smell their breath, I hadn't been detected. I started to feel pretty happy with myself, as it appeared my gamble had paid off. I was sure that I was getting some great photographs, and nothing bad had happened as the two back in the car had warned it would. I looked back at them and gave a cheeky wink, which they later said looked like I was trying to get mud out of my eyelashes. Then Salvador took a step forward.

Her tree-trunk legs plunged into the deep water, which was head deep for me but barely reached her bosom. The seismic strides sent small tsunamis that sloshed over me, chilling me to the bone and rinsing off some of the mud. She was far more stoic about the cold than I had been, but what distressed me most was that she apparently was going to cross. The herd would follow, and fifty or so individual elephants, amounting to more than two hundred legs, would soon be stomping and squelching through the place where I was lying. No matter how relaxed this herd might be, they were still wild elephants, and if I stood, the adults would react to the sudden threat and trample me, stabbing into me with their tusks for good measure. If I stayed put, I would almost certainly get trod upon and drown in the mud. Neither was appealing to me, and when Salvador gave the rumble that meant "Let's go," I knew I had to act. I slithered as inconspicuously as I could *toward* the elephants—and the deeper water.

My new plan was to stay underwater, swimming between the legs of the ellies if need be, holding my camera safe and dry above the surface like a parody of the Loch Ness monster.

As for my great fear, crocodiles, I comforted myself with the thought that the multiton animals plowing up the water would drive them away. I plunged under, my left wrist held high and the fingers of my right hand crossed, as I knew my crocodile theory was optimistic at best. A massive leg stood solidly in front of me, remarkably clear in the tannin-stained water. I snuck my face above the surface, took a breath, took a photo, and went back under. I popped up again and again and eventually realized that the elephants must know that I was there.

This revelation, and the corollary that they thought I was harmless and so wouldn't hurt me, gave me a surge of confidence. I wanted to swim openly among them as I once had with tame elephants in Asia. Then I thought of the trust they had placed in me—how lucky I had been—and took my last photos quietly. Then I slipped downstream so as not to bother them anymore.

I didn't see them again that day, and soon after, BK said he had seen them traveling south, out of the Mombo area. Salvador would lead them where they needed to go, and I couldn't wait until she brought them back.

Other elephant herds came and went in the months that followed, but they had a wary wildness to them, easy to see in the way they held themselves as I approached. I could not get as close and would never have tried swimming with them or attempted what I did the next time Salvador and her family came to Mombo.

I found the group ambling along and felt a surge of fondness for them, which doubled when I saw that Salvador's daughter (easily recognized as she had inherited her mother's buck teeth) had had an addition since she had last been with us. The little chap was already walking confidently but still had little control over the many thousands of muscles in his trunk. It swung like a rubber hose under too much pressure, on occasion so violently that it would startle him and send him scurrying to his mother for protection.

Like every other guide or wildlife lover who is eventually eaten or trampled, I felt that I had a bond with this herd that would make me safe with them. I wanted to try my luck again. So I forewent the sacred nap that I usually had between morning and afternoon drives and went straight back to find them as soon as I had no tourists to look after. They were island hopping, moving between the clusters of vegetation that grow in perfect circles throughout the Okavango. These vegetated patches were not true islands in that they were surrounded by grass, not water, and their centers were often barren, white earth with only the occasional scrubby palm as a sign of life. It was in one of these low trees that I insinuated myself, in the dead center of an island that the herd seemed most likely to visit next.

My vehicle was parked about sixty feet away, but soon offered no escape route as the elephants entered the island and started energetically eating everything they could—tearing off branches, uprooting grass and delicately tapping it against their heel to remove the dirt, and shaking palm trees to make their hard nuts fall. These tennis ball–size nuts are popped whole into the mouth, rolled like a Gobstopper, then with a resounding crack popped open by molars the size of a baby's head. The air was filled with sounds like rifle pops and grinding machines, with the occasional trumpet from a young one as it darted between an adult's legs or played chase with a cousin.

The palm cluster that sheltered me was too small to bear fruit, and the leaves held no nutrition, so the elephants didn't bother with it. On occasion they would brush by, and I would hold my breath at their enormity, their potential for violence, and their present restraint. I felt awe, respect, and something else. What I had felt before was like a crush on a pretty girl in a magazine, distant and intangible. The close contact they had allowed me had made this bloom into a type of love—that most unpredictable and dangerous of sentiments.

Then Salvador's grandson walked by, his trunk whipping

around like an epileptic snake, and he almost ruined the party. On an errant swing, his little member pushed aside the frond that was my main concealment and left me exposed to the herd.

The baby stood facing me, and I saw the first little buds of its tusks, the points squirting sideways. "Hey little guy," I mouthed, not daring to speak. "Don't tell your mum I'm here, okay?"

He stepped backward, his hind feet tangling, and as he tottered he whirled, his trunk whipping over his shoulder and hitting him on the opposite cheek. He panicked and made an un-elephantine squeak as he ran to his mother.

As one, the herd responded to his distress, stopping their feeding, dropping the branches or grass they held, raising their trunks, flaring their ears, and standing tall. His mother got to me first. The branch that I had delicately pulled back to cover me was thrust aside once more, and the world's largest forehead pushed to within a yard of my face. The circus smell of hay was overwhelming as I noted the sparse but tough bristles that sprouted from her wrinkly skin.

I should have believed I was going to die, but I didn't. I just smiled and sat still. Salvador's daughter turned her head slightly and looked at me, her eye expressing a wisdom I have found in few humans. Then she withdrew her head, the branch fell back, and I heard Salvador say, "Let's go." I didn't see them again for another six months.

■ ■

It was vultures that led me to Salvador's herd the last time we met. I had seen them circling—not an uncommon sight, but in a rush they began dropping from the sky. I pointed the vehicle in the direction they were headed. Lions, hyenas, leopards, and safari guides all follow plunging vultures, knowing that if they land during the day it is only for meat. They had dispersed through a number of trees, and I couldn't tell exactly where they were aiming.

"This is good!" I explained to my guests. "If they are landing in the trees, it means there is still a predator on the ground that won't let them get close! It's a fresh kill!" An elephant trumpeted nearby, and I wondered if it hadn't stumbled across the kill and hoped I wasn't missing out on seeing some interspecies action. Elephants sometimes chased lions, just because they could, and it was always fun to watch. I steered the Land Rover around a group of trees and found a whole herd of elephants, clearly distressed. Their ears were flared, their tusks held straight out, and they were kicking up dust and shaking branches.

The lions at Mombo were far from being brave enough to go after an elephant (in fact, with such an abundance of antelope to eat they rarely went after anything more risky than a zebra), so I explained to my guests that I didn't think it was a kill anymore.

Then my explanation was cut short, because an elephant charged us.

She emerged from the group—ears pinned flat, trunk down to protect it from impact—at a speed that is terrifying to behold. The ground rumbled, the vibrations even greater than those of the thankfully running engine. I slammed the car into reverse. This was not a mock charge.

The elephant was instantly recognizable by her outward curling tusks. Unlike Salvador, these were yet to form a full cursive W. This was Salvador's daughter, an elephant normally so calm that she had forgiven me for frightening her baby. Now she was coming fast, and as I reversed, the turbo whining, the guests bouncing on and off their seats, I thought of the only reason I could as to why she would be so upset.

"Oh no. Not Salvador." I didn't think that Salvador had been old enough to die naturally (elephants in the wild live to about sixty). A snake may have bitten her, but I couldn't believe that such a wise woman would fall to something as lowly as that. But the herd had formed a protective cluster, just as they do around a downed family member, and Salvador was nowhere to be seen.

I'd seen this in the short space of time before we ignobly fled, but the daughter gave up the chase and wheeled back to the group. The vultures squabbled and cackled in the trees. I tried to explain to my guests that there was not a kill here, just a tragedy, when the elephants parted for a moment and I saw a red stain on the ground.

And I grinned.

"Okay, that was the second time I was wrong." I said to the guests. "Get out your binoculars, we're about to see something that I've never seen before."

Every now and then the herd would shift slightly, showing Salvador standing, legs splayed, straining with her labor. After about twenty minutes there was another gush of blood, the vultures gabbled at the sight, and a baby plopped with little ceremony to the ground. It was immediately cleaned by one of its expert aunties, who had acted as midwife throughout the process.

A great trumpet came from the elephants, as if in celebration, echoed by us on the vehicle, many of whom were in tears (and that unashamedly includes me). The baby sat looking bewildered at its ejection after twenty-two months in a comfortable womb, then started comical attempts to get up. Its ears were still plastered to the sides of its head, making it look like a squat sea lion, and it moved in the same humping legless manner.

After half an hour the baby stood, to more cheering from our vehicle. And it seemed to spawn a celebration from the elephants as well, as they started picking up dust and spraying themselves with it. This coats their skin and helps protect them from parasites, but each blast knocked the little baby down, and she (by now I had seen that it was a girl) struggled valiantly back to her feet and watched the enormous battleship-gray cruisers that were in a paroxysm of excitement around her.

Salvador moved over the baby to shelter her, and the little one lifted her mouth to a nipple and took her first drink, her eye rolling the whole time, taking in the colors and movement of her new world. Eventually she stopped drinking and took her first wobbling steps. I felt like a proud parent and made encouraging noises as she tottered and fell. Her big sister, who had returned to her usual placid ways, helped her up, only to see her knocked down by an excited youngster who had run over to see what was going on. The culprit was spanked away, and the baby was led to water. And to my astonishment, only an hour after labor, Salvador swam across.

I thought of the blood in the water, and that it could attract nothing of good intentions. The lagoon they were crossing was home to some very large crocodiles that I couldn't see, meaning they were most likely lurking under the water. A baby elephant is unable to use its trunk, so I knew that the baby couldn't snorkel.

It plunged in after its mother, flanked by curious teens, and went straight under. Then it bobbed up and sank again. Every time the baby rose for oxygen, its triangular lower lip puckering and gurgling at the air, I thought, I'll give it thirty seconds, and if it doesn't come up, crocs or not, I'm going in after it. I had one foot out the car and was ready to perform the most suicidal act of a foolish life when the baby emerged from the depths, turned, and dog-paddled in a circle. It was having fun! Now I wanted to admonish it, but Salvador took over, reaching her trunk in and gently drawing the baby out of the water.

The herd crossed, and I knew we couldn't follow. I felt more privileged than after any wildlife experience. I was proud of Salvador, proud of her older daughter, and proud of the baby. Elephants don't have royalty, but I was sure that at some point, many years from that day, she would grow up and lead the herd, and I hoped that some future guide would know just how special she was, even if she did have funny teeth.

Big Mistake

I should never have quit guiding and accepted the promotion that made me a camp manager. I wasn't good at it. It also was apparent to me that people only speak to managers when they are unhappy, unlike guides, who are told quite often how great they are. But my main problem as a camp manager was with animals—or the lack of them. While I still lived in the bush, I wasn't out and about in it every day, and I craved the experiences with wildlife that I had become used to in the preceding years.

So when Chedu, a trainee manager, came and said there was an elephant between the guest tents and the main area and some people wanted to get past it, I jumped at the opportunity for some interaction.

The camp was built to the same formula as many others. It had a dining area and dinky little curio shop, bundled together with a deck, and an office for the managers. On either side of this main building, trailing off like outspread arms, were the paths that led to the guest tents. The path had handrails made from eucalyptus trees, chosen because they grow straight and hard.

This camp had the benefit of being set over a beautiful and busy lagoon that was a popular drinking spot for baboons, kudu, zebras, and the region's abundant elephants. The main area and the tents faced this never-ending and spectacular show, but the animals sometimes stepped off stage and came straight to the audience, with potentially disastrous consequences if not given quick directions elsewhere.

I set out to prompt this elephant away from the area used by the tourists. He was between the first tent and the office, so I didn't have far to go. Straight away I could see it was a young male, either in his teens or early twenties, who may have only recently left his birth herd to make it as an adult. He was decimating a fever-berry tree that shaded our plunge pool, tearing off branches and feeding them into one side of his processor-like mouth, so they emerged stripped of leaves and the valuable cambium layer of bark on the other side. A whittler could never be as neat, or quick. Watching him from the pool deck was a delighted Dutch tourist, pale and hirsute in his swimwear, looking for all the world like hairy tofu. He held a camera in his pudgy fist, and every time he snapped I saw the elephant wince. I realized that the elephant was nervous, but like a young human male was trying not to show it.

I intended to direct him toward the bush, through a wide gap in the path. This gap was specifically for elephants and hippos, so they wouldn't knock over the eucalyptus rails when they took a shortcut to or from the lagoon.

"Hey!" I said to the elephant, which had been surreptitiously watching me since I stepped out of the office. At the same time, the tourists in Tent 1 stepped out of their front door to watch, keeping it open in case they needed to dash back in. I had hurried out to face the elephant, and, perhaps rusty from my lack of guiding, hadn't looked at the situation from the elephant's perspective. I did now, and knew that I had made a big mistake.

The elephant's way to the path break on his left was now blocked (in his line of sight anyway) by the people standing outside of Tent 1 and its imposing structure. Behind him was the lagoon. And while elephants can swim, they don't view it as a means of escape. On his right was the solid structure of the main area that even an elephant would have difficulty bringing down. In front of him was the easiest path, and the only thing blocking his way was me. I suddenly felt isolated and very teeny.

In two quick strides he came and loomed over me. I had stepped back one pace at the realization of my error, but my hips had banged against the rail behind me. The elephant now had his knees against the opposite rail, only a yard and a half away. His breath smelled of hay and crushed leaves. His eyes rolled, and I knew that he was as scared as I was.

We held our standoff for a while, the only sound was the ominous creaking of the pole as he shifted his weight. If it gave way he would topple on me. If he just pushed it, he would go through as easily as I would push over a limbo pole, and I was not athletic enough to flip over the railing behind me in time should I need to.

"Oh well done genius, what are you going to do now?" It was my co-manager. Like most males, I hate being caught in a mistake, but now was not the time to give a snappy reply. I didn't respond, didn't even look at her, but could see in my peripheral vision that a small crowd of staff and guests had gathered outside the office to watch the show.

The young bull stepped back a bit, and I let my breath out. He stood tall, and I knew what was coming. Just after an elephant stands tall, they give you a display to see if you will flinch. He shook his head, his ears slapping on each side of his face, showering me with dust. Then he did something I hadn't seen before. One of the reasons I love elephants so much is that they always show you something new, but this was a trick I didn't appreciate. He added to his standard ear flap by swinging his head to the side, whipping his trunk hard and fast on a horizontal plane. It was at the level of my neck.

By now the hairy Dutchman had thought to start filming my little adventure, in case something happened that he could sell to a network, he later told me frankly. What he showed me was that I was more flexible than I would have thought. As the trunk whipped, my instincts took over and I threw myself backward. But with my hips pinned by the rail, I didn't fall. Instead I bent in the middle. My feet stayed on the ground, my upper body doing all the flexing and draping me backward over the rail. The muscular trunk would have broken my neck if it connected, and the short tough bristles on it would have gashed my skin.

It missed, though, and the elephant took another step back, then ran forward, stepped sideways, and took off through the gap in the rails.

I unfolded myself, gasping as my vertebrae tried to put themselves back into the places they were meant to be. Then I walked away from the cynical applause that had started outside the office.

I was angry with myself for making such an amateurish error. I knew too much about animals to get caught out like that.

The anger dissipated as the adrenalin left my system, and I felt my ears pushed back by a huge grin. Despite the fear, despite the embarrassment at my mistake, I had enjoyed myself during the encounter.

I went back into the office and wrote a note to the Maun office saying that I quit.

I then asked if they had any jobs going for a guide.

Epilogue

After seven years of living in a tent, I was promoted. I'd been a guide for most of those years, briefly (and unsuccessfully) tried being a camp manager, and finally inherited my friend Cliffy's grandly titled position of guide training manager and head guide coordinator when he moved on. I spent a year teaching and knew that my next step up would be an office job, probably in Maun. I would still be involved with the bush but not living in it every day. Instead I would go to an office every morning, deal with harassed camp managers over the radio, and hear secondhand about what the wildlife was up to. It didn't appeal to me at all, and I was too tired of failing to make Germans laugh to go back to full-time guiding.

So I left the company I was working for, left my many friends (both human and four- legged), and left the bush. If I was going to be in a town, I wanted it to be a real one. Since leaving I have been dissatisfied with most jobs I have taken, but I have been lucky enough to live in Sydney, Los Angeles, and San Francisco. As much as I have liked those places, I felt like I was withering without wildlife.

In 2003 I came out of guiding retirement and spent three months leading safaris in the deserts of Namibia, which included getting lost with Cliffy in the sand dunes of the Skeleton Coast, and decided to lead a few safaris every year from that point on. Now, through the Africa Adventure Company in Florida and the Classic Safari Company in Sydney, I get to go back every year and see what the animals are up to, run into some old friends, and maybe get some new stories.

Peter Allison is a safari guide who has spent much of the last twelve years leading wildlife-viewing and ecotourism trips in Africa, mostly Botswana. His love of animals led him to train as a

safari guide in the early 1990s and soon thereafter he was hired by southern Africa's largest operator to train all of their safari experts. Safaris he has led have been featured in magazines such as *Vogue* and *Condé Nast Traveler.* He has assisted *National Geographic* photographers and appeared on television shows such as *Jack Hanna's Animal Adventures.*

DANNY MASSA, DIVINITY PHOTOGRAPHY

Peter is also active with the Athena Foundation, a nonprofit conservation group. He is on the board of the Athena Foundation's youth program, whose mission is to inspire young people to develop their interest in conservation.

Originally born and raised in Sydney, Australia, he currently divides his time between Australia, California, and Botswana.